# The Pleiadians Files

Annotated references for serious
researchers of the Pleiadians, other
extraterrestrials, why they're visiting us,
and the worlds they come from.

## Volume One

# Hidden and Ancient
# Records

compiled by

Dace Fitzgerald Allen

Pleiadians Files

PleiadiansFiles.com

2010

Cover design by Dace Fitzgerald Allen.  Pleiades photo by John Stauffer (Spitzer Science Center, Caltech) Credit: NASA/JPL-Caltech/J. Stauffer (SSC/Caltech)

Any trademarks, service marks, or product names are assumed as the property of their respective owners, and used only for general reference.

DISCLAIMER

This information in book is provided only to inform and entertain.  Information is based on personal experience and research, and anecdotal evidence. It should not replace legal, medical, religious or other professional advice. Readers assume full responsibility for use of the information in this book.

ISBN-10 1456339486  / ISBN-13: 978-1456339487

Body, Mind & Spirit / UFOs & Extraterrestrials

First edition, November 2010

## The *Pleiades, by Arthur Adams*

LAST night I saw the Pleiades again,
Faint as a drift of steam
From some tall chimney-stack ;
And I remembered you as you were then :
Awoke dead worlds of dream,
And Time turned slowly back.

I saw the Pleiades through branches bare,
And close to mine your face
Soft glowing in the dark ;
For Youth and Hope and Love and You were there
At our dear trysting-place
In that bleak London park.

And as we kissed the Pleiades looked down
From their immeasurable
Aloofness in cold Space.
Do you remember how a last leaf brown
Between us flickering fell
Soft on your upturned face?

Last night I saw the Pleiades again,
Here in the alien South,
Where no leaves fade at all;
And I remembered you as you were then,
And felt upon my mouth
Your leaf-light kisses fall!

The Pleiades remember and look 'down
On me made old with grief,
Who then a young god stood,
When you—now lost and trampled by the Town,
A lone wind-driven leaf,—

Were young and sweet and good!

## Table of Contents

This book is dedicated to those from whom this information originated and to whom it refers, and their concerns for the well-being of people on this planet.

It is also dedicated to the many researchers whose writings and messages were "lost" or hidden for more than a century or, in some cases, *many* centuries.

The author gratefully acknowledges the multitude of spiritual and intuitive people whose commitment to their beliefs has left -- and continues to leave --  an important and indelible mark on our spiritual history.

Their work is honored and carried forward today, through the tireless efforts of those who believe and the beacons they provide.

Thank you.


-- D. F. A.

# Introduction

'...the gray
Dawn and the Pleiades before him danc'd,
Shedding sweet influence.'

-- John Milton, *Paradise Lost*

My personal search for ancient, historical information related to the Pleiadians (or Pleiadeans) began when I learned that the Pleiades' position in the night sky signals the end of the harvest season. Though a shift in the Earth's axis has affected the date, it's still around Halloween.

According to the astronomer describing this to me, that particular position of the Pleiades is the *single most important* astral sign of the season. In early society, that event marked the year's end, *not* December 30th.

This galvanizing discovery elevated the importance of the Pleiades in my historical search.

For many years, I'd met profoundly spiritual and intuitive people who'd explained the Pleiadians and their importance to our planet.

However, it took several years for me to discover that the Pleiades -- and the Pleiadians -- have been revered by *global* cultures throughout history.

From Asia to Africa to Europe, and from Polynesia to the Americas, people have *always* placed great importance on the Pleiades. That seems strange, logically, since the Pleiades seem like a relatively small (but bright) cluster in the night sky.

There *had* to be more to the story.

Was this information hidden from us, or simply "lost " as technology replaced cultural traditions?

Throughout my years as a researcher, I've seen that many important facts are 'hiding in plain sight' in folklore and legends. *You just need to know what you're looking for.*

> This is similar to the people of Ireland referring to their fairies -- including the Tuatha De Danann -- as 'the little people.' Earliest eyewitness accounts of the fairies indicate that most of them are anything *but* little. In fact, many of them are eight feet tall or taller.
>
> By calling them 'the little people,' the Irish felt that they were protecting themselves from the wrath of these entities who might not want to be talked about.
>
> In fact, reading some descriptions of the Pleiadians as tall, Nordic aliens, I wondered if the Tuatha De Danann were (or are) Pleiadians. I'll discuss that later in this book.

As I read the writings of Homer, Hesiod and Ovid, and legends associated with the origins of the Pleiades, I saw consistent themes woven through the stories. They parallel some (but not all) of the modern-day descriptions of encounters with -- and messages from -- the Pleiadians.

There's a wealth of information hiding in these ancient and obscure resources.

This book is the first in a series to give serious researchers a reliable library of information. For insights as well as credibility, it's important to have a solid foundation in both fact and folklore related to the Pleiades and the Pleiadians.

In the pages of this book and those that follow it, you'll find references and starting points for your own research. It's an exciting journey.

Throughout this book series, I've cast a wide net from prehistory to modern times, trusting you to 'connect the dots' between one theory and another.

For me, this is like 'The Secret' but on a different energy plane, with a somewhat different message.

Though I heartily disagree with some historical interpretations and unenlightened contexts for this knowledge, I think *all* of it is a well of vital information about the Pleiadians' role throughout Earth's history.

I've included some information that may not make sense to you when you first read it. You may ask yourself, 'Why is this here?'

It's there for a reason. It provides another research clue. It's another path that may uncover more important information about the Pleiadians.

Most of this is 'hidden in plain sight'. It's there for truly *perceptive* people -- like you -- to understand.

I'm sharing the information that I consider most important. I hope it's of value to you as a research tool that can lead to astonishing discoveries.

They light a clear path from ancient times to the future.

D.F. Allen

## Overview

This book is organized into several sections.

First, we'll talk about the traditional, scientific views of the Pleiades star cluster.

Then, we'll discuss facts and folklore related to the naming and traditions of the Pleiades. Within those tales -- and sometimes well-hidden -- you may see references to what we now believe about the Pleiadians.

It's possible that those ancient tales and records -- including passages from religious texts such as the Bible -- represent the views and guidance of the Pleiadians, put in a context suited to our long-ago ancestors.

In this book, that information has been loosely organized geographically and by culture. Look for the running themes and messages throughout those disparate accounts. <u>They're important.</u>

*Note:* Many of my references are quoted from early editions of 19<sup>th</sup> century books. I noticed that later editions of the same books significantly reduced the amount of background information related to the study of the Pleiades and Pleiadians. *That's the same information we need,* as serious researchers.

<u>Why was it removed from those texts?</u>

For example, an early version of Smith's *Bible Dictionary* provides *a full page* of details about the

Pleiades and their significance. A later edition reduced that same information to just *two sentences*.

The rest of Smith's earlier information was dismissed as -- and I quote -- 'a relic of the lingering belief in the power which the stars exerted over human destiny.'

That's the kind of information that's being lost, and one of the many reasons I compiled this book.

After reviewing ancient information about the Pleiades, we'll see how the Pleiades has been a calendar reference for people throughout time and around the world.

Finally, we'll explore some recent scientific discoveries about the Pleiades star cluster, and what it might mean to our research and our future.

With this foundation in historical and scientific Pleiadian research, you'll be well equipped to see what's important in more *recent* discoveries about the Pleiadians and their contact with us.

You'll also be able to counter skeptics' efforts to trivialize the work of serious Pleiadian researchers, and the people whom the Pleiadians contact.

## What are the Pleiades?

The Pleiades is a star cluster located in the constellation of Taurus.

The nine brightest stars of the Pleiades are named for the Seven Sisters of Greek mythology: Sterope, Merope, Electra, Maia, Taygete, Celaeno, and Alcyone, along with their parents Atlas and Pleione.

The cluster has sometimes been called the Maia (or Maya) Nebula, named after the star, Maia.

A few people have called it the Plough, but that's usually the nickname of Ursa Major, also known as the Big Dipper or Saptarishi.

In astronomy, the Pleiades, or Seven Sisters (also called Messier object 45), are an open star cluster.

In addition to hundreds of faint stars in the cluster, the Pleiades contain middle-aged hot B-type stars. Class B stars are *extremely* luminous and blue.

The Pleiades cluster is among the nearest star clusters to Earth. It's usually the cluster most obvious to the naked eye in the night sky.

## Pronunciation

The word 'Pleiades' has many pronunciations in English. Mostly, it varies with the person saying the word, but here are some general guidelines by region.

In America and Canada, it's often pronounced PLEE-uh-deez. You'll also hear some Americans say it PLEE-ay-deez or plee-AY-deez. Some Canadians (and a few Americans) pronounce it PLAY-uh-deez.

In the U.K., it's generally pronounced PLY-uh-deez. Australians often say it similarly.

## Age of the Pleiades

According to Earth scientists, the Pleiades cluster was formed about 100 million years ago, when dinosaurs were still a dominant life form here. (By contrast, Earth's sun is about five *billion* years old.)

Some Pleiadians would disagree with that those time estimates.

Reflective dust around the brightest Pleiadian stars was first thought to be left from the formation of the cluster. It's now known (or claimed) to be an unrelated dust cloud in the interstellar medium that the stars are currently passing through.

Astronomers estimate that the Pleiades cluster will survive for about another 250 million years. Then, they believe it will disperse due to gravitational interactions with its galactic neighborhood.

## Distance to the Pleiades

The distance to the Pleiades cluster is an important first step in what's called the *cosmic distance ladder,* a sequence of distance scales for the whole universe.

The size of this first step calibrates the whole ladder, and the scale of this first step has been estimated by many methods. As the Pleiades cluster is so close to the Earth, its distance is relatively easy to measure.

This allows astronomers to plot a Hertzsprung-Russell diagram for the cluster. Then, when compared to clusters whose distance is not known, their distances can be estimated.

In other words, the distance to the Pleiades cluster is the standard used to measure the distance to all other star clusters, galaxies and clusters of galaxies.

Ultimately, astronomers' understanding of the age and future evolution of the universe is influenced by their knowledge of the distance to the Pleiades.

The Pleiades have been measured at about 135 parsecs away from Earth, or about 440 light years.

Strangely, the Hipparcos satellite measured the distance at only 118 parsecs. That's *over 55 light years closer to us* than previously measured.

Later work has consistently found that the Hipparcos measurement was in error, but it is not yet known why the error occurred... or if it even *was* an error. All they know is that, *at that moment in time*, the Hipparcos measurement didn't match the usual numbers.

Did the Pleiades cluster actually *move* for a short time? That's no more unlikely than some other beliefs about the cluster and its inhabitants.

The cluster core radius is about 8 light years and the tidal radius is about 43 light years. The cluster contains over 1,000 confirmed members, excluding unresolved binary stars.

Young, hot blue stars dominate the Pleiades cluster. Some believe that they're too volatile for habitation. Up to 14 of those stars can be seen with the naked eye.

The arrangement of the brightest stars is somewhat similar to Ursa Major and Ursa Minor. The total mass contained in the cluster is about *800* solar masses.

The cluster contains many brown dwarfs, not heavy enough for nuclear fusion reactions to start in their cores and become proper stars.

Astronomers have made great efforts to find and analyze brown dwarfs in the Pleiades, because they are still relatively bright and observable. Brown dwarfs in older clusters have faded and are much more difficult to study.

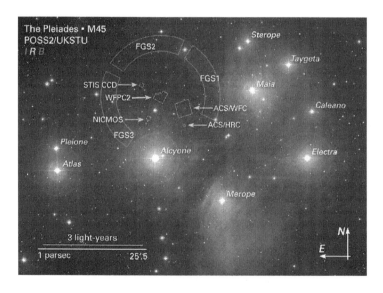

Annotated NASA photograph of the Pleiades

Most NASA photos in this book are courtesy of
NASA/ESA/AURA/CalTech.

## Pleiades in modern popular culture

Science fiction

- In *Foundation* and *Empire* by Isaac Asimov, a soldier is described as coming from the 'agricultural worlds' of the Pleiades. The implication was: They provided cannon fodder for the army in the days of the Galactic Empire.

Video games

- One image of the Pleiades was selected for the cover art of the US release of *Xexyz* video game.
- The Pleiades are also referenced in *Persona 2* with the name of 'Seven Sisters High School', which some of the characters attend.
- In *Super Smash Bros. Brawl*, the Lylat Cruise stage is situated on an original spacecraft that doesn't appear in the Star Fox series called *Pleiades.*

Music

- Mentioned in the Red Hot Chili Peppers song 'Can't Stop'.
- Mentioned in the song 'Emily' by Joanna Newsom
- There is a song entitled 'Pleiades' on *Gretchen Goes to Nebraska,* the sophomore offering from progressive metal/tribute band King's X.

Other

- Subaru is the Japanese name for the Pleiades star cluster, which inspires the logo for the Subaru brand automotive manufacturer .

### Who are the Pleiadians?

The Pleiadians inhabit, originated at, or are based in or near the Pleiades cluster.

Most researchers will agree with that. From that common ground -- no pun intended -- many differing opinions emerge.

---

**Important:** <u>The following notes barely scratch the surface of these issues. They are not complete and are **not** intended to endorse any one set of beliefs over another.</u>

They're simply a *sampling* of diverse views so readers will understand the complexity of this subject.

---

Many people classify Pleiadians as Aliens, Type 3: Human-Type Aliens.

Some, including X-Files enthusiasts, further distinguish them as Human Type-B Aliens. That means they're similar to Human Type-A Aliens ('Blonds') but different from Human Type-C Aliens, usually hailing from Sirius.

Others believe that Blonds and Nordic Aliens are different Pleiadians.

*Note:* The term 'Pleiadians' has been attributed to the messages transmitted through Billy Meier in the 1970s, though the spelling associated with his work is Plejaren. According to a 1995 message, the Plejaren cluster is about 80 light years beyond the Pleiades.

Other messages suggest that some Plejarens originated on the planet Erra, which revolves around the star, Taygeta, in the Pleiades cluster.

Are Plejarens the same entities that others call Pleiadians? It *seems* likely but that's far from certain.

Some people believe that Pleiadians are humanoid and share a common ancestry with us, through the Lyrans. In fact, all humanoid inhabitants of our universe may be descendants of the Lyrans, from the 12th dimensional stargate known as Lyra.

 Scientific studies support this possibility. For example, Nobel Prize winner Dr. Francis Crick -- one of the co-discoverers of the structure of the DNA molecule -- speculated that our DNA could have come from space.

According to Wikipedia, 'In the early 1970s, Crick and Orgel (a noted British chemist) further speculated about the possibility that the production of living systems from molecules may have been a very rare event in the universe, but once it had developed it could be spread by intelligent life forms using space travel technology, a process they called 'Directed Panspermia."

Some people say the Pleiadians only *appear* to us in human-like form, so we can identify with them. In fact, the Pleiadians may inhabit a fifth (or higher) dimension where form is more fluid.

Others say Pleiadians may be manifesting on our planet as dolphins or mermaids.

In general, people who believe in the Pleiadians regard them as evolved beings that are able to communicate with people on Earth, directly or telepathically. Some believe that the Pleiadians are benevolent beings monitoring and protecting our planet and its people.

According to many who place spiritual significance on Earth's relationship with the Pleiadians, the Pleiadians operate on pure intention. That intention -- or its spiritual vibration -- is generally interpreted as love.

In addition, others -- including Barbara Hand Clow -- describe nine levels of awareness or dimensions of consciousness that the Pleiadians hope to convey and share with us.

Several others have received messages that are similar but either build on that concept, clarify it, or give a different viewpoint with a similar theme.

Some people believe that the Pleiadians live in a realm that is our next evolutionary step, as well.

Other believers are less comfortable trusting the Pleiadians, and carefully evaluate all messages sent to Earth, and those that convey them.

Many believers are confident that Pleiadian starships are circling our planet right now. Some say the Pleiadians visit us in physical form. Others are equally certain that the connection is channeled or telepathic, and -- in some cases -- manifests as physical form so that we can more readily accept its reality.

In Volume Two of this series, *The Pleiadians Files: Vril Research,* I'll document some of the deeper significances of the Pleiadians, their technology and their messages, and their possible relationships with the people of Earth.

However, it's not my intent to summarize the works of *modern-day* researchers and channelers. The Pleiadians Files are generally references providing academic *historical* and *background* information for easy use by researchers and students.

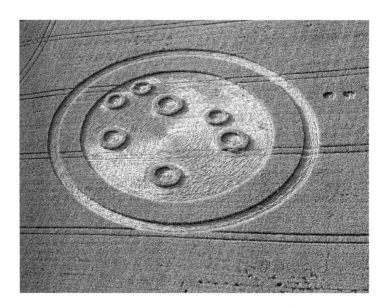

Pleiades Crop Circle, Froxfield

Wiltshire, England, ca. 1994

## Do the Pleiadians visit Earth?

The simple answer to the question, "Do the Pleiadians visit Earth? " is "Yes. " That's what many people believe, and -- in later chapters of this book -- you'll see many references that seem to confirm it.

In more recent times, particularly from the 19th through the 21st centuries, specific incidents are reported.

One of the most poignant appears in the book, *Angels and Women.* In this passage, the fallen angel, Hesperus, points to a star cluster (assumed as Pleiades) and refers to it as his ancient realm:

"O Aloma, beautiful, beloved, look forth into the western sky. Seest thou the brightest of yon celestial group, a star radiant and tender as thine own eyes? There once I dwelt, happy and pure. I would return unto mine ancient realm. I have seen thy soul, Lily of Light, and I tire of earth, its baseness and sin. "

In the foreword of that book, editor/reviser

Mrs. J. G. Smith quotes the Bible:

"For God spared not the angels that sinned, but cast them down to hell, and delivered them into chains of darkness, to be reserved unto judgment. " (2 Peter 2:4.)

"And the angels which kept not their first estate, but left their own habitation, he hath reserved in everlasting chains under darkness unto the judgment of the great day. " (Jude 6.)

She then comments:

"Since the flood these evil angels have had no power to materialize, yet they have had the power and exercised it, of communicating with human beings through willing dupes known as spirit mediums. Thus have been deceived hundreds of thousands of honest people into believing that their dead friends are alive and that the living can talk with the dead.

"All students, familiar with the Bible teaching concerning spiritism, will read this book with the keenest interest because it shows the method employed by Satan and the wicked angels to debauch and overthrow the human race.

"The reviser of this book is of the opinion that the original manuscript was dictated to the woman who wrote it by one of the fallen angels who desired to return to divine favor. "

Clearly, she is concerned about the safety of people communicating with spirits, including those who receive messages from the Pleiadians.

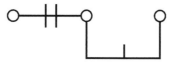

The bigger questions *may* be:

- Do we regularly encounter Pleiadians <u>and not realize it?</u>
- When did they first begin visiting Earth?
- Technically speaking, are we *all* descendants of the Pleiadians, and therefore Pleiadians ourselves?
- What distinguishes Pleiadians from other extraterrestrials?
- What can we learn from and about the Pleiadians and related extraterrestrials?

## Pleiadians' Earthly relatives and descendants

Information received by respected experts such as Barbara Marciniak explain that the Pleiadians are our relatives from eons ago.

Some say that our shared ancestors are the Lyrans of the northern constellation, Lyra, of which Vega is the alpha star.

## The Lyran connection

Though the written history of the Lyrans (or Lyrians) isn't as complete as records related to Pleiades, stories continue to reference the constellation Lyra and its brightest star, Vega.

For those who believe that Lyra is the birthplace of the humanoids in the Milky Way, history is sometimes complex and conflicting.

Some, including Lyssa Royal and Keith Priest, authors of *The Prism of Lyra* , describe a group consciousness called the Founders. The *Prism* authors agree that this group has also been called the Watchers, Eternals, Reflectors and Seeders.

They talk about Lyra being the general area from which the humanoid race was born.  Lyra is our ancestral connection with the other members in our galactic family.

Those family members -- sometimes called the Lyran Group -- *may* include species from Sirius, Orion, Alpha Centauri, Altair, Earth, the Pleiades, Vega, Zeta Reticuli, and other related planets and stars.

The humanoid Lyran forms include Caucasians, giants (six to nine feet tall, such as the Tuatha De Danann), redheads (may include giants), darker-skinned humanoids, birdlike Lyrans, and those that resemble cats.

Some of our brightest writers and scientists have been dropping hints about Lyra.

Heinlein's novel, *Have Spacesuit - Will Travel,* Lyra/Vega include a planet with an advanced civilization. It is the local overseer of the Three Galaxies federation, and the curator of humanity after its discovery by the Three Galaxies.

In the original Star Trek series episode, *Tomorrow is Yesterday,* the Vegan Tyranny is mentioned. *Space: 1999* included androids from Vega. *Babylon 5* has a Vega Colony.

Even in more modern media, Lyra is regarded as a possible home for higher intelligence. The movies *K-PAX* and *Contact* -- based on Carl Sagan's novel of the same name -- both movies identified Lyra and/or Vega's realm as inhabited.

An Internet search on Vega in fiction will provide a larger and newer list, as more writers, artists and scientists are referencing Lyra and Vega in their work.

### Other stars and planets

Many related planets and stars are identified as inhabited or a home to extraterrestrials who visit and/or contact people on Earth.

Aldebaran is one of the more famous, with references in the *Lord of the Rings,* Lovecraft's *Cthulhu Mythos,* E.E. Smith's *Lensman* series, Ursula Le Guin's novels, the *Hitchhiker's Guide* books, and many other classics.

Even Thomas Hardy, in *Far From the Madding Crowd,* mentions Aldebaran and the Pleiades.

Generations have grown up familiar with Aldebaran, thanks to its regular reference in various *Star Trek* series.

When we note the consistent interest -- by some of our brightest minds -- in the Pleiades and nearby planets and stars, one has to wonder if there's a genetic memory or a galactic consciousness at the core.

The lines between fact and fiction, fantasy and history, begin to blur.  The likelihood of a "lost " history becomes more probable.

That history is echoed in Earth legends from many cultures that indicate a specific and clear genetic connection with the Pleiadians.

For example, some people believe that early (and perhaps current) members of the Cherokee nation came to Earth from the Pleiades; their 'starseed' legends indicate that heritage.

However, cultures around the world have revered the Pleiades and included their history in their beliefs and practices.

In the next chapter, we'll explore some of the best documented evidence for this.

## The Pleiades - A Global Tradition

If there is a written tradition from any part of the world, it usually includes veneration of the Pleiades.

According to Schaff-Herzog, 'The **Pleiades** (*Sibitti*, ' the Seven ') were worshiped in Babylonia, and the name occurs in incantation texts as that of a group of demons (Schrader, *KAT*, pp. 413, 459), possibly represented in Canaan by Beersheba; in this case the word is wrongly etymologized as ' well of swearing ' (Gen. xxi. 30, xxxi. 33).'

Later, this book says:

"In China among the objects of imperial worship at the capital are the **Pleiades**, the five planets, and the constellations, as well as the starry China heavens as a whole.

"The high ceremonies of this worship take place at the winter solstice at the Temple of Heaven situated in the southern part of the Chinese city of Peking. There are tablets to the souls of these bodies, as well as to the sun and the moon, which last are included in the worship.

"In the common or popular religion these bodies have either a far less prominent place or none at all, though certain heavenly bodies which superstition connects with wind and rain receive special attention.

"These bodies are supposed to be the agents of the Yin and the Yang, the male and female elements of the universe.

"The star-cult in Japan, so far as early testimony (the Nihongi) is concerned, is confined to the star-deity Amatsu mike hoshi (' dread star of heaven ') or Ame no Kagase wo (' scarecrow male of heaven '), a malignant god who was vanquished in the cosmic battle between forces malign and benign (for control of man), and to Vega and the North Star, whose worship came from China (W. G. Aston, Shinto, p. 142, London and New York, 1905). The worship of the malign deity was probably avertive.

"Similarly in India the worship of Saturn is that of a malignant and dreaded deity, who is propitiated by sacrifice.

"The indications of star-worship among primitive peoples are elusive and unsatisfactory, and the most that can be said with certainty is that much of the material is rather that of folk-lore and mythology than of ritual.

"Yet it may be noted, for example, that the Berbers offer worship to Venus, the **Pleiades**, Orion, the Great Bear, and the Little Bear.

"For some details of folk-lore, cf. J. G. Frazer, Golden Bough, ii. 19 sqq. (London, 1900). "

We'll revisit these passages later in this book.

*Universal Brotherhood* magazine described another group that places significance on the Pleiades:

"The sun and moon figure as secondary deities among the Mincopies. They do not appear to worship them, but (like the Bushmen) honor them with certain observances. The Bushmen also celebrate the rising of the **Pleiades** with something like a religious festival.

Though both divisions of the Pygmy race do not appear to worship trees or rocks, yet they seem to attach significance to certain localities legendary or traditional. Moreover, the Bushman hails the rising of the sun by a few moments of silent meditation, paid in a solitary spot, just before dawn. "

The following passage is lengthy. Some of it may seem murky and will require much cross-study with ancient mythological traditions. However, I think you'll see how the Pleiades (and the Pleiadians) are an important root of many (perhaps even most or all) mystical and religious traditions throughout Asia, Polynesia, Europe, the Middle East and parts of the African continent, and the Americas.

In *The angel-messiah of Buddhists, Essenes and Christians,* by Ernst von Bunsen, the author says the following.

According to Pherecydes (about B.C. 544), or rather according to the ' Phoenician' tradition to which he referred, the fundamental cause of all phenomena in nature is Zeus or Chronos, whom he also calls, but distinguishes in a certain sense from Chthon, that is, the material substances of the earth, including the sea.

He designates Chronos as a deity, dwelling in that part of heaven which is nearest to the earth.

We know that Chronos is the Seb of the Egyptians.
With Khea-Netpe he gave birth to the five planets, in
honour of which, five additional days were added to the
calendar of 360 days.

After that Thot, the God of history and astronomy --
who is represented as riding on the moon, and whose
mystical number was 72 -- had played at dice with the
moon, and gained for each planet the 72nd part of 360
days.

This Egyptian legend seems to have been framed after
the Phoenician legend or myth of <u>the seven children of
Chronos and Rhea</u>, of which the youngest had been
translated to the Gods. Movers has explained these
seven children of Zeus-Chronos by the **Pleiades**, one
of which seven stars had disappeared in
course of time.

Since Pherecydes admits to have drawn
from a Phoenician source, he must have
known this Phoenician legend, and he
may be assumed to have connected with
the seven sons of Zeus-Chronos the
<u>seven Pataeci of the Phoenicians, and the
Cabiri of Egyptians and Greeks</u>, whom
some identified with the sons of Rhea.

Zeus-Chronos thus seems to have been
by Pherecydes connected with the
**Pleiades** in Taurus, <u>as the divinity dwelling in these
seven stars, like the Sibut of the ancient Babylonians,
the Sebaot or Zabaot of the Hebrews, and other deities</u>.
This hypothesis is confirmed by other details about the
theogony of the tutor of Pythagoras.

The first creation of Zeus-Chronos was fire.

According to the Indian myth on the descent of fire, the same was brought to earth from heaven by a messenger of Indra, by Agni, called the Matarisvan.

This name, Mr. Haliburton, of Nova Scotia, has connected with the Matarii, as the **Pleiades** are still called by islanders in the Pacific.

We have pointed out in another place, that the fire-sticks or Arani' of the Indians, which were a sacred symbol to the ancient Babylonians, point to the origin of the Cross as connected with the symbolism of fire.

It can be shown that Bel's flaming sword which turned every way, and the flaming sword of the Cherub, that is, Kirub or bull, according to the language of Cuneiform Inscriptions, originally referred to the **Pleiades** in Taurus, from whence fire was supposed to have first descended upon the earth.

The connection of the Cross with fire receives a remarkable confirmation by the Chinese symbol of the 'headless cross' or Tau.

It becomes increasingly probable that the Chinese interpretation of the cross symbol is more ancient than the provable introduction of the same into other countries. For ' it is now asserted by one of our best Sinologists (Dr. Edkins), that the phonetic roots of the Chinese language are the same as those of Europe; in other words, that the Chinese phonetic roots are those from which the languages of Europe, and therefore of India, were originally developed.'

Among the earliest and simplest ideographic symbols in the Chinese language is one which resembles precisely our capital letter T, without the final strokes, signifying that which is ' above,' and the converse of this, the T resting on its base, signifies that which is 'below.'

In both cases a point or a comma, as if a tongue of fire, is added, as similarly in Europe a dot or tongue of fire is placed occasionally over an angel or divine messenger, to signify his more than human character.

This dot, as signifying fire, is clearly pointed out in the symbol for fire itself in the Chinese language, and it is this: a piece of wood boring into another piece, and on the opposite side a spark issuing, indicating the generation of fire by friction.

Now, the dot as signifying fire was placed, as Agni was placed by the Indians, in a place of pre-eminence over the visible world.

Hence, connecting this idea with that of the former, with the symbol for height or heaven, we have the complete idea represented symbolically of the supreme power pictured as fire or a spark presiding over the lower world, and so placed above it.

This symbolism is visible everywhere.

In Egypt we find the well-known ' <u>key of the Nile' in the hand of Isis</u>, denoting simply the supreme power exercised by that divinity.

<u>The same symbol in China denotes the supreme Lord or Ruler of the Universe</u>, and is, in fact, a part of the expression used to signify ' God.'

We have here, then, one of the earliest inventions of man by which is denoted something ' above,' that which is visible to the eye, or ' heaven.'

When solar-symbolism took the place of fire-symbolism, the sun's disc took the place of the fiery tongue, and thus originated the so-called handle-cross of the Egyptians, the symbol of life.

As symbol of life it is represented without the circle under the nostrils of a Pharaoh, whilst a line connects the Tau-cross with the sun or solar disc. Thus was expressed in an Egyptian figure or symbol, similar to one of the Chinese, how the God whose symbol was held to be the sun, breathed into the nostrils of man ' the breath of life.'

The Papal crozier has exactly the same form.

The reversed Tau-cross, symbol of the lower world, with the Chinese perhaps the most ancient of the two, may be regarded as having referred in the first place to the horizontal balance of aboriginal times.

That connected the two determining single stars on the horizon, like Aldebaran and Antares, by Indians called 'rohin' or red, no doubt because the rising and the setting sun made them appear red.

According to this hypothesis, the vertical line of this symbol would date from a later time, and would point to the vertical balance, formed by the culminations of these determining stars.

<u>These three points in the sphere formed the very ancient holy triangle, which in the Holiest of the Holy in the Jewish Temple was represented by the Shechina in the midst and above the two Cherubim, and which later was connected with the Divine Trinity in Unity.</u>

If the astronomical origin of this Oriental symbolism is proved, as also its introduction in the West in preMosaic times, it may be unhesitatingly asserted that the connection of Zeus-Chronos by Pherecydes with that part of the earth which was nearest to ' heaven,' points to the above astronomical symbolism.

...The light hemisphere seems to have been originally regarded as the spiritual world ; <u>but special constellations, later the sun, were regarded as the dwelling-place of the God who causes the order in the universe, and as centre of the spiritual world</u>.

This symbolism enables us to suggest that Pherecydes -- the first person to write in Greek about nature and the gods -- may have regarded as dwelling-place of Zeus-Chronos the Eastern determining star of aboriginal times, Aldebaran in Taurus, or the **Pleiades** in the same constellation.

...Since the seven sons of Zeus-Chronos and of Rhea, according to Phoenician legend were, as we showed, connected with the **Pleiades**, this constellation, inhabited according to Old-Babylonian and to Hebrew tradition, by the God Sibut-Sebaot, appears indeed to have designated the part of the earth which was conceived to be nearest to heaven and the dwelling-place of Zeus.

For the **Pleiades** stood once nearest to the most ancient equinoctial points observed, and the parts of the sphere determined by the latter mark those points on the horizon where the path of the sun appears to touch the path of the fixed stars, and at the same time the equator, and thus the earth. This explanation is finally confirmed by the fact to which Pherecydes refers, that Zeus-Chronos was the creator of fire and then of the earth, as if the creator of heaven and earth, whilst the Pleiades, as already said, were regarded as the locality where fire originates.

In order to frame the world, Zeus transforms himself into Eros, the god of love, not mentioned in the Homeric Poems, but whom the Orphics before Pherecydes explain to have been the son of Chronos, and the first who issued forth from the mundane egg.

Eros was thus connected with Castor, the first-born of the Dioscuri, who were called sons of Zeus and Leda.

Since the Dioscuri can be connected with the Aswin, or two Bulls of Indian tradition, with the rising and setting Taurus -- to which also Osiris and the Cherubim and Seraphim were referred -- the argument gains in force, that Zeus, who was called the highest, like Osiris-Wasar, according to the most ancient Greek theogony known to us, <u>was supposed to be the God inhabiting the **Pleiades** in Taurus</u>.

Eros became the vicar of Zeus and the framer of the world, and <u>so Serosh took the place of Ormuzd as first of the seven Amshaspands, which referred to the Pleiades</u>.

Like Eros, Serosh was considered as the framer of the world. Again, as Serosh-Sraosha <u>was connected with the celestial watchers, and thus with the **Pleiades**</u>, being therefore opposed by the ideal hero in the opposite constellations of Scorpio or the Serpent, the adversary of Eros is the serpent-deity Ophioneus.

Eros must therefore be regarded as one of the ideal heroes of light, who were connected with the constellation of the spring-equinox, originally with Taurus and the **Pleiades**, and opposed by serpent deities.

Eros was contrasted to Ophioneus as Ormuzd was to Ahriman, Indra to Ahi, Osiris to Typhon, Dionysos to the serpent-footed Titans, Apollos to Python, Buddha to Mara (Naga), Christ to Antichrist, the satan, devil, or old serpent.

The localisation of these Eastern and Western symbols enables us to assert that the theogony of Pherecydes, and therefore also of Pythagoras, was inseparably connected with astronomical observations of the East. It is certainly not only the myth of Demeter and of Dionysos, the Indian Bacchus, which can be proved to have been introduced into Greece from without.

The Orphic cosmogony, which is more ancient than Pythagoras and his tutor, confirms our explanation of the Greek theogony as based on astronomical observations of the East, and on the symbolism connected with it.

Chronos, the fundamental principle, creates the opposing principles of light and darkness, the aether and the chaos, from which Chronos forms a silver egg, from which again issues forth the enlightening Phanes, who is also called Eros and Metis, that is, Wisdom, the Greek Sophia and the Indian Bodhi.

The Sophia was later designated as daughter of Okeanos and Thetis. The latter already Hesiodus mentions as the first consort of Zeus, who devoured her, at the suggestion of Gaea and Uranos, in order to prevent the birth of a Divine being. Zeus caused Athene, symbol of the morning dawn, to issue forth from his head.

The statue and temple of Athene (Athena) were turned towards the middle dawn of the equinoxes, a trait of the myth which confirms the astronomical character of the earliest known nature-symbols, and the connection of Greek philosophy with Eastern astronomy and symbolism.

We are now in a position to assume that already centuries before Pythagoras, the Initiated among the Greeks, the epopts, were taught in and through the mysteries a more speculative theology, <u>a deeper knowledge or gnosis, to which the so-called Gnomons referred by dark sentences, riddles, or proverbs</u>.

From this it would follow that, through the Mysteries, secret doctrines of Oriental priests could be transmitted to Greek philosophers, which through them reached the public.

All Greeks were admitted to the representation of the mystic symbols, but these were not intended for the education of the people, and not explained to them. Moreover, there were certain ceremonies to / which only the Initiated were admitted.

Even without having travelled to the East, Pythagoras, the contemporary of Buddha, could have. It will become more and more probable that he had a knowledge of Eastern wisdom.

*The Transmigration of Souls.*

The connection of the Pythagoraean doctrine about the transmigration of souls with the Dionysian Myth confirms in the most absolute manner the direct connection between Greek philosophy and Eastern astronomical symbolism.

Pythagoras is said to have been the first who taught this

doctrine in Greece, the first traces of which occur among the Brahmans and Buddhists. According to the Buddhistic 'Tradition from beyond,' the Bodhi, or Wisdom from above, was personified by angels and by men, and the spiritual power or Maya, the Brahm, was also called the Word, or the Holy Spirit.

From time to time an Angel is designated in his turn to be born in the flesh, and to teach as the enlightened man, as Buddha and as Saviour of the World, the wisdom which he has brought from the upper and spiritual to the lower and material world.

This incarnate Angel-Messiah, after having fulfilled his mission, returns to the upper spheres, his transformations, his deaths and births, his change of body, what the Greeks called 'meteusomatosis,' have come to an end for him, and he enters the locality, the characteristic feature of which is Nirvana or destruction, that is, the annihilation of matter.

This last resting-place of the spirit, where the harvest takes place, is the abode of the spirits perfected before him, and also the dwelling-place of the self-existent deity, Isvara-Deva.

Nirvana is the sun.

The doctrine of the incarnation of the Angel-Messiah or Buddha, his birth in the flesh as the last of a series of births, was connected with the doctrine of the soul's transmigrations, and thus with a concatenation of bodily existences.

Each of these formed a new prison for the soul, which was held to be of heavenly, of immaterial, of spiritual origin.

According to Egyptian conception the soul had to migrate from the lowest animal to the highest, and thus had to become embodied by men as well as by higher beings of other stars. The graduated scale of the soul's transformations was by the Egyptians connected with the Phoenix period.

The Phoenix-bird or Phenno is by Herodotus described as most like an eagle, and every 500 years, as he was told, the young bird buried the old bird at Heliopolis.

At Heliopolis was the Mnevis or black Bull with the white sign of an eagle (Phenno) on its back. <u>This Bull with the mark of the Phoenix can be proved to have referred to the celestial Bull, to the constellation of Taurus</u>, which in the East rises on the horizon as 'the living Apis,' and sets in the West as 'dead Apis' or 'Bull of the West.'

The places on the horizon which are marked by the rising and setting Taurus, like those marked by the new moon and the full moon, and which were called ' the two eyes' of the moon-god Thot, were held to be ' the two heavenly gates,' between which the migrations of the soul were conceived to take place according to the Book of the Dead.

So also <u>Osiris, originally the God in the **Pleiades**</u>, had to migrate through the fourteen moon-stations of the lower sphere before he could rise again in the East with the **Pleiades** in Taurus as the God in the **Pleiades**, in order to recommence his rule in the fourteen moon-stations of the upper hemisphere.

The connection of the Pythagoraean doctrine about the transmigrations of the soul with Dionysian or Bacchic rites is generally acknowledged, and is as certain as the connection of the Dionysos Myth with that of Osiris.

<u>These myths must be connected with the East and astronomically interpreted, if the localisation of these and similar nature-symbols has been established.</u>

Assuming this, it follows that the connection of Pythagorean conceptions with provable astronomical observations and symbols of the East can no longer be doubted.

Among the ideal heroes of light which, like Osiris and Dionysos, were connected with the spring-equinoctial constellation, and were opposed by ideal heroes of darkness inhabiting the constellation of the autumn equinox, was also Buddha, the contemporary of Pythagoras.

<u>Because Buddha was symbolised by the sun, he was represented as Lamb, referring to the spring-</u>

equinoctial sign of Aries in his time, which rose on the horizon at his birth.

Even the expectation of the coming Buddha was connected with this Eastern astronomical symbolism.

The expectation of his birth on Christmas-day, and at midnight, is connected with a symbolism which is much more ancient than the time of Gautama-Buddha.

*The Goddess Hestia.*

We saw that the creator of fire, as later of sun, moon, and earth, that Zeus-Chronos throned in the **Pleiades** according to the theogony of the tutor of Pythagoras, and that according to Indian tradition the Matarisvan, the messenger of Indra, sent from the Matarii or **Pleiades** to the earth, that Agni, whose secret name was Matarisvan, was held to have brought the fire and the fire-sticks to the earth.

With these Oriental conceptions of Pherecydes the statement may be connected, that the Pythagoraeans placed the fire goddess Hestia in the centre of the universe.

We may assume that Pythagoras knew for what reason the sun had taken the place of fire as symbol of the Divinity. Pythagoras could regard the sun as the centre, though not of the universe, yet of the solar system, with which he seems to have been acquainted.

This hypothesis is confirmed indirectly by the place which the Pythagoraeans seem to have assigned to the earth as to the second moon, perhaps because the moon accompanies the earth in its rotation round the sun, both receiving their light from the latter.

Pythagoras could assign to the sun the central position in the solar system, without giving up the Oriental connection of the fire with <u>the **Pleiades**, the latter as the throne of the God by whom fire had been sent.</u>

From this the conception would arise of the Pleiades, or a star in this constellation, as the throne of Hestia and as centre of the universe.

It is remarkable that, according to the calculations of the astronomer Maedler, <u>the earth's sun appears to rotate round a star in the **Pleiades.**</u>

More important still is it for our purpose, that according to statements made by Cicero and Plutarch about astronomical conceptions of some Pythagoraeans, especially of Aristarchos from Samos, who flourished from about B.C. 280 to 264, Copernicus, led by these ideas, as he himself seems to imply, separated the equinoctial points from the solar path, and thus may be said to have re-established the most ancient and absolutely exact year of the East, which was regulated by fixed stars.

From the intricate, woven themes of the Pleiades throughout spiritual and mythical history, I think you can see that there is very solid evidence to point to the importance of the Pleiades -- and perhaps the Pleiadians -- as the source of knowledge (and certainly the gift of fire) for early man.

In the next passage, let's revisit the information from the Schaff-Herzog encyclopedia, and see where this leads us in understanding the important role of the Pleiades in global history, mythology and spirituality.

From *the Schaff-Herzog encyclopedia of religion:*

Similarly, and perhaps consequently, Jupiter, Mars, Mercury, and Saturn took the same prominence in their nightly places as the sun in its corresponding positions, and were compared with that body in its relative importance.

The **Pleiades** *(Sibitti,* 'the Seven ') were worshiped in Babylonia, and the name occurs in incantation texts as that of a group of demons (Schrader, *KAT,* pp. 413, 459), possibly represented in Canaan by Beersheba; in this case the word is wrongly etymologized as ' well of swearing ' (Gen. xxi. 30, xxxi. 33).

The sun, moon, and Venus were thought of as in control of the zodiacal signs, and so of all the influences that effect on the earth increase and decay, light and darkness, cold and heat, life and death. <u>In Egypt star-worship was, in historical times, not that of the star itself but of the divinity conceived as animating it</u>.

That this is a developed conception is at once evident, and points to the earlier belief in the life and divinity of the heavenly body itself.

The fact of Egypt a certain type of star-worship is established by the figuring of the deities of Jupiter, Saturn, Mercury, Mars, and Venus as mounted on their boats (this fixes their divine character, as it is the Egyptian method of representing the journeyings of the gods and corresponds to the Babylonian method referred to above, where deities are riding various animals), and making their progress under the guidance of Orion and Sirius (E. Lefebure, *Les*

*Hypogees royaux de Thebes,* part 4, plate xxxvi., Paris, 1886).

So there was a Sothis or Isis-Sothis, the deity of Sirius or the Dog Star. But <u>the notice of such divinities is rare,</u> and invocation of them is not frequent.

Excerpts from *A classical dictionary* by Charles Anthon:

ALCYONE, or HALCYONE, I. daughter of Aeolus, married Ceyx, who was drowned as he was going to consult the oracle. Tile gods apprized Alcyone in a dream of her husband's fate; and when she found, on the morrow, his body washed on the seashore, she threw herself into the sea.

To reward their mutual affection, the gods metamorphosed them into halcyons, and, according to the poets, decreed that the sea should remain calm while these birds built their nests upon it.

The halcyon was, on this account, though a querulous, lamenting bird, regarded by the ancients as a symbol of tranquillity; and, from living principally on the water, was consecrated to Thetis.

According to Pliny (10, 47), <u>the halcyons only showed themselves at the setting of the **Pleiades** and towards the winter-solstice</u>, and even then they were but rarely seen. They made their nests, according to the same writer, during the seven days immediately preceding the winter-solstice, and laid their eggs during the seven days that follow. These fourteen days are the '*dies halcyonii,*' or ' halcyon-days,' of antiquity.

...

II. A daughter of Atlas, and one of the **Pleiades**. (*Vid.*
Pleiades. — *Apollod.,* 3, 10.)

III. An appellation given to Cleopatra, daughter of Idas
and Marpessa. The mother had been carried off, in her
younger days, by Apollo, but had been rescued by her
husband Idas, and from the plaintive cries which she
uttered while being abducted, resembling the lament of
the halcyon, the appellation *Alcyone* was given as a
kind of surname to her daughter Cleopatra.

...

ATLANTIDES, a name given to the daughters of Atlas
They were divided into the Hyades and **Pleiades**.

ELECTRA, I. one of the Oceanides, wife of Atlas, and
mother of Dardanus by Jupiter. *(Ovid, Fast.,* 4, 31.)

II. A daughter of Atlas and Pleione, and one of the
Pleiades. *(Vid.* Pleiades.)

III. One of the daughters of Agamemnon. Upon the
murder of her father, on his return from Troy, Electra
rescued her brother Orestes, then quite young, from the
fury of Aegisithus, by despatching him to the court of
her uncle Strophius, king of Phocis. There Orestes
formed the well-known attachment for his cousin
Pylades, which, in the end, led to the marriage of
Electra with that prince.

According to one account, Electra had previously been
compelled, by Aegisthus, to become the wife of a
Mycenean rustic, who, having regarded her merely as a
sacred deposite confided to him by the gods, restored
her to Orestes on the return of that prince to Mycenae,
and on his accession to the throne of his ancestors.

Electra became, by <u>Pylades</u>, the mother of two sons, Strophius and Medon. Her story has formed the basis of two plays, the one by Sophocles, the other by Euripides.

[IN A REFERENCE TO HERCULES:]

The constellation of Orion, who was fabled to have pursued, through love, the **Pleiades**, or daughters of Atlas, now sets: the herdsman, or conductor of the oxen of Icarus, also sets, as does likewise the river Eridanus. At this period, too, the Pleiades rise, and the she-goat fabled to have been the spouse of Faunus.

Now, in his tenth labour, <u>Hercules restores to their father the seven **Pleiades**</u>, whose beauty and wisdom had inspired with love Busiris, king of Egypt, and who, wishing to become master of their persons, had sent pirates to carry them off.

HYADES, according to some, the daughters of Atlas and sisters of the **Pleiades.** The best accounts, however, make them to have been the nymphs of Dodona, unto whom Jupiter confided the nurture of Bacchus. (Consult *Guigniaut,* vol. 3, p. 68.) Pherecydes gives their names as Ambrosia, Coronis, Eudora, Dione, Aesula, and Polyxo. *(Pherecyd., ap. Sclud, 11., 18, 486.)*

Hesiod, on the other hand, calls them Phaesula, Coronis, Cleea, Phaeo, and Eudora. *(Ap. Schol. ad Arat., Phaen., 172.)* The Hyades went about with their divine charge, communicating his discovery to mankind, until, being chased with him into the sea by Lycurgus, Jupiter, in compassion, raised them to the skies <u>and transformed them into stars</u>. *(Pherecyd., I. c.)*

According to the more common legend, however, the Hyades, having lost their brother Hyas, who was killed by a bear or lion, or, as Timaeus says, by an asp, were so disconsolate at his death, that they pined away and died; and after death they were changed into stars. *(Hygin., fab.,* 192.—*Muncker, ad loc.)*

The stars called Hyades derived their name from *vo,* '*to make wet,*' '*to rain,*' because their setting, at both the evening and morning twilight, was for the Greeks and Romans a sure presage of wet and stormy weather, these two periods falling respectively in the latter half of April and November.

On this basis, therefore, both the above legends respecting the Hyades were erected by the poets. In the case of the nymphs of Dodona, the Hyades become the type of the humid principle, the nurturer of vegetation; while in the later fable, the raindrops that accompany the setting of the Hyades are the tears of the dying daughters of Atlas.

The Hyades, in the celestial sphere, are at the head of the Bull. The number of the stars composing the constellation are variously given. Thales comprehended under this name only the two stars *a* and *e*; Euripides, in his Phaelhon, made the number to be three; Achieus gave four; Hesiod five; and <u>Pherecydes, who must have included the horns of the Bull, numbered seven.</u>

The scholiast on the Iliad, however, gives only the names of six Hyades, when quoting from the same Pherecydes, the name of one having probably been dropped by him; for the Atlantides were commonly reckoned as amounting to fourteen, namely, <u>seven **Pleiades** and seven Hyades.</u>

MAIA, daughter of Atlas and Pleione, and the mother of Mercury by Jupiter. She was one of the Pleiades; and the brightest of the number, according to some authorities: others, however, more correctly make Halcyone (Alcyone) the most luminous.

PLEIADIS I. the daughters of Atlas aid the ocean-nymph Pleione. They were seven in number, and their names were Maia, Electra, Taygela (Taygeta), Halcyone, Celseno, Sterope, and Merope, The first three became the mothers, by Jupiter, of Mercury, Daidanus, and Lacedsemon. Halcyone and Celeno bore to Neptune Hyrieus and Lycus; Sterope brought forth Oenomaus to Mars; and Merope roamed Sisyphus.

These nymphs hunted with Diana; on one of which occasions Orion, happening to see them, became enamoured, and pursued them. In their distress they prayed to the gods to change their form, and Jupiter, taking compassion, turned them into pigeons, and afterward made them a constellation in the sky.

According to Pindar, the Pleiades were passing through Bceotia with their mother, when they were met by Orion, and his chase of them lasted for five years Hygmus (I. c.) says seven years. *(Keightley's Mythology, p. 464.)*

The constellation of the **Pleiades**, rising in the spring, brought with it the spring-rains, and opened navigation. Hence, the name is thought to indicate the stars that are favourable to navigation.

Ideler, however, thinks it more probable that the appellation is derived from the Greek, full, denoting a cluster of stars; whence, perhaps, the expression of Manilius calls the **Pleiades** 'moving in seven paths', although one can only discern six stars.

Hence Ovid says of these same stars *(Fast., 4.170),* *'Quae septem dici, sex tamen esse solent.'*

On the other hand, Hipparchus asserts, that in a clear night seven stars can be seen. The whole admits of a very easy solution.

The group of the **Pleiades** consists of one star of the third magnitude, three of the fifth, two of the sixth magnitude, and several smaller ones. It requires, therefore, a very good eye to discern in this constellation more than six stars. Hence, among the ancients, since no more list six could be seen with the naked eye, and yet since, as with us, a seventh star was mentioned, the conclusion was that one of the cluster was lost. Some thought that unit been destroyed by lightning; others, making the lost Pleiad to have been Electra, fabled that she withdrew her light in sorrow at the fall of Ilium, and the misfortunes of her descendants, Urdanus having been the son of Electra and Jupiter.

According to another account, the 'lost Pleiad' was Merope, who withdrew her light because she was ashamed of having alone married a mortal.

Others, again, affirmed that the star in question moved away from its own constellation, and became the third or middle one in the tail of the Greater Bear, where it received the name of 'the Fox.' *(Ideler, Sternnamen, p. 145.)*

From their rising in the spring, the **Pleiades** were called by the Romans *Vergilae. (Festus.— Isidor., Orig.,3,* 70.) This constellation appears to have been one of the earliest that were observed by the Greeks. It is mentioned by Homer *(Il.,* 18, 483, *seqq. — Od.,* 5, 272, *seqq.)*; and in Hesiod an acquaintance with it is supposed to be so widely spread, that the daily labours of the farmer can be determined by its rising and setting.

...Some have been led into the erroneous opinion, that the name of the constellation was derived from *"pigeon"* or *"dove"* in allusion to the fancied appearance of the cluster. *(Schwenk, Mythol. Skizz., p.2)*

The **Pleiades** are assigned on the celestial sphere to a position in the rear of Taurus. Proclus and Geminus, however, place them on the back of the animal; while Hipparchus makes them belong, not to Taurus, but to the foot of Perseus.

II. The name of **Pleiades** was also given to seven tragic writers, and the same appellation to seven other poets, of the Alexandrean school.

...

To the poets of the Alexandrean age belong Apollonius the Rhodian, Lycophron, Aratus, Nicander, Euphorion, Callimachus, Theocritus, Philstar, Phanocles, Timon the Phliasian, Scymnus, Dionysius, and seven tragic poets, who were called the Alexandrian Pleiades.

...

PLEIONE, one of the Oceanides, who married Atlas, king of Mauritania, by whom she had twelve daughters, and a son called Hyas. Seven of the daughters were changed into a constellation called **Pleiades,** and the rest into another called *Hyades. (Ovid, Fast., 5,84.)*

From *The ruling races of prehistoric times in India...,* by James Francis Katherinus Hewitt:

Indian ritual tells us of a time when the Neshtri, the successors of the consecrated maidens of Istar and the village dancers, the priests of the supreme god Tvashtar were not unsexed, while their associate the Agnidhra, or priest of the fire-god, was like his brethren elsewhere, an unmanned priest, and the sign of duality, *tva,* in the name of Tvashtar seems to denote the age of his supremacy as that <u>before the worship of the fire-god when time was measured by the **Pleiades** year of two seasons.</u>

...

It was among the worshippers and sons of the goddess Sar that the astronomical computation of time, the stages of which I have traced in Essays m. and iv., began. And it was they who framed the myth of the twin children of Saranyu, the goddess Sar, the twins Day and Night, originally born on the osier and poplar-lined river Xanthus, the yellow river of Asia Minor, the mother-river of the yellow race.

It was they who, in Greece, worshipped the goddess Sar, not only as the mother of the later Erinnyes, but as the twin Charites who bear her name (khar=sar), the two seasons of the year of <u>the **Pleiades**, who were the first supreme local gods of Sparta.</u>

...

**Other notes**

From Wikipedia:

The Alexandrian Pleiad is the name given to a group of seven Alexandrian poets and tragedians in the 3rd century B.C. (Alexandria was at that time the literary center of the Mediterranean) working in the court of

Ptolemy II Philadelphus. The name derives from the seven stars of the Pleiades star cluster.

Alexeander [sic] was a very intelligent poet who believes that all of mankind was evil and based many of his true feelings of life in poetry.  He believed we should all be ruled with absolute monarchy and that no one on earth was born good or should be trusted. All were born evil.

There are several conflicting lists of the greatest poets of the Alexandrian age (traditionally ascribed to Aristophanes of Byzantium and Aristarchus of Samothrace) which include the "Alexandrian Pleiad ", some with tragic poets, other which include lyric or epic poets.

The following members are usually included in the "Alexandrian Pleiad ":

> * Homerus the younger, son of Andromachus, from Byzantium, a tragedian who wrote 57 plays

> * Philiscus of Corcyra

> * Lycophron

> * Alexander Aetolus, tragic poet

> * Sositheus of Alexandria, dramatist

> * Aeantides, a poet traditionally associated with the "Tragic pleiad "

The other members are variously:

> * Theocritus, who wrote the bucolic poems

* Aratus, who wrote the Phaenomena and other poems

* Nicander

* Apollonius, who wrote the Argonautica

* Sosiphanes of Syracuse, tragic poet

## Later use

The name "Pléiade " was adopted in 1323 by a group of fourteen poets (seven men and seven women) in Toulouse and is used as well to refer to the group of poets around Pierre de Ronsard and Joachim du Bellay in France in the 16th century (see "La Pléiade ").

Also, the **Pléiade** is the name given to a group of 16th-century French Renaissance poets whose principal members were Pierre de Ronsard, Joachim du Bellay and Jean-Antoine de Baïf.

In modern times, "pleiad " is also used as a collective noun for a small group of brilliant or eminent persons.

The name Pleiades has also been applied to natural features, especially rock formations, cascades and waterfalls.

One is near Warren, NH, by Mt. Moosilauke and the Jobildunk ravine.

Another describes a canyon route that references seven waterfalls in Moab, Utah.

**The Pleiades in Native American Lore**

In *The test-theme in North American mythology,*
author Robert Harry Lowie explains the following.

XI. STAR-MYTHS.

Applying the principle thus gained to the study of star-
mythology, we ask:

Are the nature-mythological conceptions which
undoubtedly have developed from observation of the
firmament the starting-point of the tales connected
with them, or have these tales developed independently
and become secondarily joined with the nature-myth
proper?

The **Pleiades** tales have been pointed out as classical
examples of nature myths, and the occurrence of such
tales in all parts of the globe has been said to exemplify
the psychical unity of mankind. Now, it need not be
denied that the nature-mythological personification of
this constellation has led to simple explanatory
statements.

The Fraser River myth reads as follows: 'Qals went on
and found a group of children who were crying because
their parents had left them. He transferred them to the
sky, and they became the Pleiades.' Here the
apperception of the Pleiades as a group of children is,
of course, the nature-myth, their transference to the
sky by the transformer may be justly considered an '
explanatorische Hinzudichtung.' But it is doubtful
whether full-fledged tales develop in this way.

In a Cheyenne story a young woman is married by a
dog and gives birth to seven puppies. Her husband
leaves with the children, and is followed by the woman.
Suddenly the tracks stop.

'She looked up, and there she saw seven pups; they were stars.'

The numerous variants of the story among the Eskimo, Athapascan, Northwestern, and Plains tribes lack the astral feature at the close.

At the same time, the number of puppies in the several versions varies considerably, from two to ten.

What has taken place among the Cheyenne is perfectly clear. The condition for the development of a **Pleiades** tale is the presence of seven actors forming a group.

In a region in which astral transformations are common the presence of a group of beings tends to amalgamate with the independently developed personification of the Pleiades, and this accounts for the Cheyenne form.

The Cheyenne story well illustrates the principle that the type of association found in a given case is to a considerable degree conditioned by the specific type, or formal setting, of plots found in a cultural area. For example, Eskimo folk-lore, as Boas has shown, is essentially human in setting. There are no complex animal tales; the strictly indigenous portion of Eskimo mythology is made up of hero-tales bearing a very general resemblance to those of eastern Asia.

On the other hand, among several Plains tribes, notably those of Caddoan stock, folk-lore tends to assume an astral aspect, while the Kwakiutl and kindred tribes most frequently relate the meeting of an ancestor with a supernatural being and the consequent acquisition of a dance or charm. We might therefore expect that in the case of widespread narratives the same tale might appear among the Eskimo in human connections, while the Pawnee version would be joined with an astral milieu, and the Kwakiutl variant with a tale of ritualistic acquisitions. This is actually the case. Among the Eskimo the story of the dog-husband is either joined with the Sedna myth, or accounts for the origin of alien tribes. In the Heiltsuk version the dog's offspring meet spirits from whom they learn the winter dance. In the Cheyenne version we found a **Pleiades** ending.

Differently from all these, the Chilcotin variant is combined with one of the typical Pacific traditions, the transformer cycle. Under the circumstances, it would obviously be a monstrous assumption that the tale of the dog-children originated among the Cheyenne as an explanation of the **Pleiades.**

We may safely assert that the story of the dog marrying a girl is the primary element in all the versions, and has in each tribe become assimilated to the conventional mould, or united with some important tribal myth.

The secondary assumption of a nature-mythological aspect is also very clear in a Pawnee tradition.

Here the rattling skull, one of the commonest features of North American mythology, is the pursuer; the heroine begs a number of animals for assistance in a series of characteristic dialogues, and creates obstacles by means of magical objects.

She is saved by several brothers, with whom she finally constitutes the **Pleiades.** The widely diffused elements making up the substance of this story occur in such a variety of different combinations that any explanatory function in connection with the observation of the stars is inconceivable.

Neither can the Shoshone tale of Coyote and his daughters, which ends with a **Pleiades** transformation, have originated in this way, for this element at the close, and the prerequisite condition that a number of characters be united in a group of six or seven, are both lacking in the Maidu, Ute, Navaho, and Pawnee versions.

In other cases, however, the nature-mythological view may, at first sight, appear equally plausible.

In a familiar Plains legend a girl turns into a bear, and after killing the tribesmen pursues her brothers, who ascend to become a constellation.

The absence of the astral element in the Coos and Ponca versions might be explained by degeneration. That this would be an artificial theory becomes manifest on examining a series of myths from a tribe whose mythology abounds in astral transformations.

For the sake of illustration, I shall briefly summarize a number of Wichita stories.

1. A woman turns into a man-eating bear and pursues her seven brothers, who ascend to the sky by means of a feather and form the Dipper.

2. Coyote, disguised as a woman, is married by seven brothers. She tries to abduct their child, but is overtaken. The brothers then form the Dipper.

3. An ogre lures a woman away. She escapes and is pursued by her husband, who is killed by a powerful old man. The wizard's seven sons marry her. The old man gets dissatisfied and takes the entire family to the sky, where they become Ursa Major and the North Star.

4. Coyote obtains supernatural power, but is warned to keep away from women. He yields to temptation, becomes an animal, and loses all his power. His

adopted son makes a formal announcement to the people of what has happened and of his intentions, and becomes the Morning Star.

5. Flint-Stone-Man goes on the war-path, ordering his wife not to send her son after him before he is of age. The youth grows up, and joins his father. The old man declares his intention of becoming the great South Star. The youth returns, summons a council, makes the formal declaration, and becomes a star like his father.

6. Poor Wets-the-Bed outdoes other warriors and wins the chief's younger daughter. His sister-in-law at first despises him, but falls in love and tempts him when he suddenly becomes handsome. He decides to go away, makes the customary announcement, and becomes a star. Most of the people become animals.

7. Child-of-a-Dog, owing to the trouble he has had, becomes a wind, his wife changes to a raccoon.

8. A chief's son marries a girl, but does not acknowledge her as his wife. She becomes an eagle and flies away with his child. Her husband then becomes an otter.

9. The hero's son is taken away by a witch. The hero stays by the water looking for his child, and after the formal announcement turns into a flamingo.

10. A young chief carries a burr-woman on his back. Turtle succeeds in shooting her off, but the old chief fears further misadventures, and after the usual declaration the entire family become eagles.

11. A man who gambles for life is beaten by Half-a-Boy, who decides to become a blackbird.

12. A bad boy reforms and becomes a powerful warrior. He remains unmarried, and finally becomes a hawk.

13. Wets-the-Bed, after performing warlike deeds, becomes a shooting-star.

The common element of all these tales is the final declaration that, owing to certain conditions or happenings, the hero has decided to assume a non-human shape.

*What* he changes into is immaterial. It may be an eagle, or an otter, or a flamingo, yet no one supposes that the tales joined with these transformations are in any way explanatory. It is quite arbitrary to select the tales with astral endings and assume that *they* are explanatory.

...We are thus warranted in concluding that in the domain of astral mythology <u>the secondary identification of a human hero with a celestial body, instead of being merely a theoretical possibility, has repeatedly occurred.</u>

...If star-myths are developed everywhere from observation of the heavens, why this extraordinary efflorescence of star-lore among the Pawnee and Wichita compared with its relative meagreness among the Eskimo and in the Northwest?

...Another factor in the development of association must, however, be recognized.

Though the connection of the **Pleiades** with the Cheyenne tale is secondary, and though the astral relations are sufficiently accounted for by the foregoing considerations, the fact that the **Pleiades** rather than, as in other versions, some other constellation or single stars, are connected with the narrative, depends on the congruity of the number of actors with the number of stars in a group.

That's a very tidy explanation but, in my opinion, it's too simplistic.

If we assume that the story was chosen *only* because the constellation had seven stars, <u>why the Pleiades?</u>

On many nights, only six of its stars are easy to see with the naked eye. There would need to be an explanation for the variable star.

The Great Bear (Big Dipper) would be a *far* better choice if the *sole* criterion for creating the legend was the number of actors matching the number of stars.

Other easier choices would include the Little Dipper (Ursa Minor), Cassiopeia and the Corona Borealis.

There's more to discover in the hidden meanings of Pleiadian lore among Native Americans.

## The Pleiades and Early Calendars

Edited from *The ruling races of prehistoric times in India, southwestern Asia, and southern Europe, Volume 1* by James Francis Katherinus Hewitt

But before closing this Essay, I must describe the method of reckoning time and fixing the dates of the national festivals used by the earliest matriarchal races, which is much older than that which appears in the story of Nala and Damayanti, and in the year of five seasons on which the plot of the Mahabharata is founded.

This method, which uses the **Pleiades** as measurers of time and the customs born from it, indubitably proves that the people who brought to Europe the Indian system of village communities, originally came either from the southern hemisphere or from countries near the Equator.

The constellation has always been associated with agriculture, and Hesiod tells us that corn is to be cut in May, when the Pleiades rise after disappearing for forty days, and that land is to be ploughed in November, the Southern spring month.

The Dyaks of Borneo regulate their agriculture by the movements of the **Pleiades,** cutting the jungle when they are low in the east before sunrise, burning what they have cut when the constellation approaches the zenith, planting when it sinks towards the west, and reaping their crops when it sets in the early evening.

Over the whole southern hemisphere time has apparently for countless ages been measured by a year of two seasons, in which the beginning and end of each season is indicated by the presence or absence of the **Pleiades** above the horizon at sunset. When the sun is west of the Pleiades during the Southern spring and summer, from November till April, the constellation is at sunset above the horizon, and when it is east of the Pleiades during the Southern autumn and winter, from April to November, the Pleiades set before the sun, and are therefore invisible at sunset.

Ellis, in his *Polynesian Researches,* tells us that the Society and Tonga islanders call the spring and summer season, beginning the year in November, *Matarii i nia,* meaning the time when the **Pleiades,** called the mother stars *(mata),* are seen at sunset, and the autumn and winter, from April to November, when they are not seen, *Matarii i raro.*

All nations in Polynesia begin their year in November with a festival to the dead, and at this season the Tonga islanders, Ceylonese, and Dyaks of Borneo, hold their feast of first-fruits, called Inachi in Fiji, and Nycapian in Borneo, and this festival corresponds with that of the first-fruits of winter rice, called Janthar-puja, kept in November by the Bengal Santals, who call one of their septs by the name of the **Pleiades**, Saren.

The Western Hindus, who trace their descent from the mother Amba, the chief star of the **Pleiades,** begin their year with the month Khartik, sacred to the **Pleiades**, in October-November, and hold their great star festival, called Dlbali or Dipavali, the feast of lamps *(dipa),* meaning that of the bright fire-gods *(vali),* in the same month, by illuminating the streets and houses, and this is reproduced in the feast of lanthorns in Japan.

The fire-worshipping Soghdians and Chorasmians of Central Asia began their list of twenty-eight lunar stations, indicating the position of the moon during each day of the lunar month, with the **Pleiades**, called by them Parwe, or the begetters *(peru),* and thus showed that the beginning of their year, regulated by these months, must once have been reckoned from the position of the Pleiades.

In America the Mexicans, who, as I have shown in Essay i., were led to the new continents by the Indian fish-god, and who brought with them to their new home the Indian and Kushite sacred symbol of the raincross, began their cycle of fifty-two years with the culmination of the **Pleiades** at midnight in November.

Then the new sacred fire, lit to replace that put out in all houses and temples, was kindled with the fire-sticks laid on the breast of the human victim, the most noble of their captives, who was sacrificed to vitalise with his blood the earth whence the sons of the new era were to be born.

Some of the most significant of the rites marking the beginning of the year of the **Pleiades** in November are furnished by the festivals of that month in the Egyptian ritual.

The Egyptians worshipped the Pleiades under the name of Athur-ai, the stars of the goddess Athyr, which was one of the names of the mother-goddess Hat-hor, and also that of the third month of their year. Hat-hor means the house or mother *(hat)* of the supreme god *(hor)* Horus, who was the meridian pole of Egyptian cosmogony, also called Amon-ra, and her name thus shows that she was from the first a time goddess.

That she was originally a goddess of the South is shown by her being the mother-goddess of the sacred tree of the South, the sycamore or fig-mulberry, called Neha; and this tree was the Egyptian counterpart of the Hindu fig-tree, the mother-tree of the Kushite race.

Her Hindu origin is also shown first by her festival of the 5th Pharmuthi, about the 19th February, a date which nearly corresponds with the great Magh festival of the Santals, Ooraons, and Mundas, to the fire and witch mother-goddess Magha, when the Santal year ends.

She was then worshipped in Egypt as the goddess Bast, distinguished by bearing on her head a lunar crescent, with the snake creeping under it.

And a second proof of her Hindu origin is given by her being the fish-goddess, to whom the Aten, or carp, allied to the Hindu Rohu of the same genus, is sacred, and also by her being in one of her forms Hat-mehit, the wife of Osiris, the goat-god of Mendes, who bore the fish sign on her head.

The Santal name for the **Pleiades**, Sar-en, is also connected with the fish-goddess, for the mother-goddess of the Savars, the Sus, the Su-varna or trading races of the West, is, as I have shown in Essay in., a fish-goddess, called Sal-rishi, a name which I have traced to the mother cloud-goddess Sar, and the father antelope *(rishya)*.

The cloud-goddess Sar was, as I have shown, the Vedic Saranyu, the mother of the twins, day and night, who still retains her place in Indian mythology as the god Hari, whose first avatar was a fish.

She was the fish-mother, also called Amba, the mother, the first star in the **Pleiades**, who led her sons, the farmers and mariners of Southern India, to Persia, Egypt, Syria, Asia Minor, and Greece, in all of which countries she was worshipped as the fish-mother.

A four days festival was held in Egypt on the 17th Athyr (September-October), the month sacred to the

**Pleiades**, about the 4th of October, to celebrate the mourning of Isis, the name given to Hat-hor, as the cow and mountain-mother *(is)*, for the death of Osiris, but that the mourning was prospective, and indicated grief for the closing year, which is to be replaced by its successor, the new year, is shown by the date of the festival of the death of Osiris.

This took place on the 26th Choiak, about the 12th November, four days after the hoeing festival, held on the 22d Choiak, and four days before that of Nahib-ka, the primaeval snake-god of the tree-worshippers, which was kept on the 1st Tybi.

 The festival of the 26th Choiak was, like the Hindu Dlbali, at the same season, the occasion of a general illumination, and then Osiris was placed in a ship, and launched out to sea.

Hence the story tells us that Osiris, the strong *(psr)* sun-god, the Assyrian Asar, worshipped both in the Euphratean Delta and Egypt as the god symbolised by the eye, showing him to be the all-seeing eye of heaven, was another form of the Akkadian Dumu-zi, the son *(dumu)* of life *(zi),* the young sun-god, who, in the original Deluge story, set forth in his bark at the summer solstice, when the Indian rains and the later Egyptian year began, to pursue his course through the seas of time, till the close of his yearly journey.

In the 26th Choiak, the day of 'the month chosen for the festival of Osiris, said by Egyptian mythologists to represent water', we see proof that the choice of the day was influenced by the science of sacred numbers, which, as I have shown above in speaking of the story of Nala and Damayanti, plays such an important part in ancient mythology.

For the number twenty-six is sacred to a lunar year of thirteen months, measured by twenty-six lunar phases; and this proves that Osiris was a sun-god, ruling the lunar year, his ship being the crescent moon, and he himself being, like Dumu-zi, the star Orion, the Akkadian Uru-anna, meaning the foundation *(uru)* of heaven, the hunter who, as I show in Essay iv., drove before him through its yearly course the crescent moon, the Indian fox, the chariot horse of India, who afterwards became the lunar hare, and which was symbolised in the constellation Lepus.

This conclusion is confirmed by a hymn supposed to be addressed by Isis to Osiris, in which she says to him—It is in the myth telling of the death and burial of Osiris that we can trace exactly how the life-giving sap, which made all plants, and the animals who fed on them, to grow, became the parent god, the eye of all living things, the god Piru, or parent god, who, in the Finnish theology, gave eyes to the snake.

He, the god of the discerning eye, who traversed the world with the ever-recurring phases of the moon, and thus made grain, fruits, and flowers to spring up under his footsteps in the lands suited to their growth.

In this story Osiris is the god of the corn-growing races, who, after having diffused through the world plenteous crops of wheat and barley, grown on fertile arable land, returns at the end of his year's course as the sun, who has done his journey.

When he returned to die as the sun of the old year he was slain by Set, his brother, whose name means, as I have shown, 'the vanquished' god, and who was really the black water-snake Ap-ap-i, and seventy-two others, representing the form of theology in which the triad of three seasons ruled by the black water-snake, the constellation Hydra, which I have described in Essay iv., the seven days of the week, and the ten lunar months of gestation, were the ruling gods.

They placed his body in a coffin, the ship which had been his cradle as the infant year, and threw it into the Nile.

Isis searched all over the world for her lost lord, and found his body on the Syrian coast at Byblus, and on looking for the coffin, found it enclosed in a pillar formed from an Erica-tree which had grown round it, been cut down and used for one of the pillars of the palace of the king of Byblus.

This was the house-pillar, the father pole of the Northern races, which I have described in Essay m., and it is this Erica-tree which was the parent tree of the Syrian races, the original barley-growers.

She took the body and the coffin, the cradle of the new god of the North, who was to supersede the god of the South, when time-measurements were based on the movements of the **Pleiades** and Orion, back to Egypt.

On her arrival she left the body mid went to visit Hor-us, the new god of the Northern house-pole, whose four sons guarded the four quarters of the heavens, the meridian pole of the Kushite race, whose revolutions were to he used as measurements of time, in place of the rising and setting of the stars.

The year thus introduced was that of four and five seasons, which I have described in Essay rv. 'While Isis was with Hor-us, Set found the body of Osiris, and cut it up into fourteen pieces, scattering them abroad, and these represent the fourteen days of the lunar phases by which time was now to be measured, the Hindu constellation of the Shishu miira, meaning the Alligator, the fourteen stars round the pole, which were

turned by the twin stars Gemini, and among these was
the star Marichi, the fire spark, the parent star of the
Kushite race.

These deductions, which make the year opened by the
**Pleiades** the first form of the year ruled by Osiris as
Orion, are confirmed by the festival held in the month
Athyr, sacred to them, to celebrate the mourning of
Isis, and in the day chosen for the festival, the 17th of
the month, we find the sacred numbers, seven and ten,
representing the seven days of the week and the ten
months of gestation.

That this number was deliberately chosen, is proved by
its being repeated in the Hebrew story of the Deluge.

In this Noah, the year god, the son of the fish-mother,
embarks on his birth-voyage, or period of conception,
on the 17th day of the second month, the Hebrew
Marchesvan, answering about to the 2d of November,
and we thus see that his voyage, like that of Osiris,
began in the same month which begins the year of the
**Pleiades**.

The year-goddess, who was born in this voyage, was the
mother mountain Ida, the cow, and mountain-mother
of the ploughing race, the Hindu and Phrygian
counterpart of the Egyptian Isis, who emerged from the
waters, according to Genesis, on the first day of the
tenth month, and, according to the Hindu story of
Manu, at the end of the birth-year.

It is she who survives in Bengal as the goddess Durga,
the mountain, under the name of Kali, meaning the
time-goddess, and her connection with the **Pleiades**
year is shown by the celebration of her festival, the
Kali-Puja, on the darkest night of the dark half of
Khartik, the **Pleiades** month.

Her altars are then drenched with the blood of goats, sheep, and buffaloes, the last being the plough animals of the Southern races, and their sacrifices show that her worship dates from the age of totemistic feasts.

But we have now to turn to another aspect of the **Pleiades** ritual, shown by the festival to the dead, celebrated, when the year began, in November.

This festival to the dead year, and to the dead who died in past years, is celebrated in the Society and Tonga Islands by prayers offered at the November New Year's Festival, for the souls of departed relatives, and its most ancient form appears in the corroboree dances of the Australian savages.

At the November midnight culmination of the **Pleiades**, called by them Mormodellic, when, as we have seen, the Mexican cycle began, they worship the dead for three days.

The Peruvians also began their year in November, and called the New Year's feast Ayu-Marca, meaning the carrying *(marca)* of the corpses *(ayu),* and they then visited the tombs of their ancestors.

The Sabaean fire-worshippers of South-western Asia held the festival, called by Albiruni the Great Bakht, or day of fate, or the first day of the month, called Murdadh by the Persians (October-November), answering to the Hindu Khartik the **Pleiades** month, and worship Venus, called Tar-sa, as the fishmother, on the 17th of the month, thus reproducing again in this series the number seventeen.

It is sacred to the Angel of Death, and on it the Festival of the Dead was celebrated.

But it is in the ritual of the Druids that we find the most certain evidence of the advent to Europe of the Southern races, who measured time by the **Pleiades**.

The Druids, or priests of the tree *(dru),* were the religious teachers of the Cymric Celts, who, according to their traditions, were led to Western Europe by the god Hu. His name, as I shall show in Essay in., is the Northern form of the root *m,* to beget, or conceive, which, again, is a Southern form of the Akkadian *Jehu,* the bird, the mother-bird, whose history I give in Essay III., and who laid the world's egg, which also appeared in their theology.

It was from this root *su* that the Indian Soma was formed, and it was in the Soma festival that the sacred sap was worshipped as the water of life, which, when sent from heaven as seasonable rain, became the essence of all plant-life.

It was thus the generator and sustainer of all material existence depending on growth and increase.

This was the god Hu who led them from India, and it was thence that, together with his worship, they brought the belief in matriarchal government, shown in the equality of the Druid nuns witli the male priests, and the birth-legend of the world's egg laid by the mother-bird, formed of snakes, from which the hundred Nagas, or rain-snakes, the Kauravya, or tortoise, sons of the goddess-mother Gan-dhari, were born.

It was also from India that they brought their reverence for groves and trees and the human sacrifices introduced by the fire-worshippers.

They celebrated the reconstruction of the world on the 1st November. As a symbol of its death and resurrection, the Druidess nuns, the priestesses of the mother-earth goddess, were then obliged to pull down and rebuild the roof of their temple. If any one of them, when bringing materials for the new roof, let her sacred burden fall, she was set upon and torn in pieces by her companions.

All fires, as in Mexico, were then extinguished, and had to be relighted by the sacred fire kindled by the Druid priests.

During the darkness of the nights after the fires had been put out, the dead of the past year were, as among the Egyptians, thought to pass to the west, whence they were carried in boats to the judgment-seat of the god of the dead, before they passed to the Elysian fields, the gardens called by the Greeks the Hesperides, the home of the maidens who guarded the three golden apples— the three seasons of the year.

These were brought each year to earth by the sun of the West and South, Hesperus, the god of the winter season, in which the young sun-god of the coming year is born.

<u>It is this Druid festival and the three days' corroboree of the Australian savages which still survive throughout Europe in the three sacred days of the 31st of October and the 1st and 2nd of November, called All Hallow Eve, All Saints' Day, and All Souls day.</u>

It is on All Hallow Eve that in Scotland, Ireland, Wales, and Cornwall torches and bonfires are still lighted and games played, and the Guy Fawkes bonfires of England are only transfers of these New Year's fires to the 5th of the month.

*A note from Wikipedia:*

Guy Fawkes Night, also known as Bonfire Night (more casually in recent times as Fireworks Night), is an annual celebration held on the evening of 5 November to mark the failure of the Gunpowder Plot of 5 November 1605, in which a number of Catholic conspirators, including Guy Fawkes, attempted to destroy the Houses of Parliament in London.

The occasion is primarily celebrated in Great Britain where, by an Act of Parliament called The Thanksgiving Act, it was compulsory until 1859, to celebrate the deliverance of the King of England, Scotland, and Ireland.

It is also celebrated in some former British colonies including New Zealand, Newfoundland, South Africa, parts of the Caribbean and the British Overseas Territory of Bermuda.

Bonfire Night was celebrated in Australia until the mid-to-late 1970s, when sale and public use of fireworks was made illegal and the celebration was effectively abolished.

Festivities are centred on the use of fireworks and the lighting of bonfires.

[Continuing the passages from *The ruling races...*]

It is on All Souls' Day that the people of France, Belgium, South Germany, and Russia visit the tombs of their ancestors, hang wreaths and light candles over their graves.

But the November festivals of the **Pleiades** were not the only important feasts of this early cult, for we find that those connected with the southern, western, and northern spring in April and May, assumed, when the village communities had finally settled in the northern hemisphere, even more importance than the November feasts of the South.

It was then that the Gonds of Central India founded the Northern spring festival of the Nagar, or plough-god, answering to the hoeing festival, the spring feast of the South, celebrated in the Egyptian Choiak (November). The name of the plough-god has been translated by the Greeks into Ge-ourgos, the worker of the earth, and the history of his worship is fully given in Essays I. and III.

It was also in April that the apparently earlier festival of the Palilia, out of which that of the plough-god grew, was celebrated. These, and the annual dances round the Maypole, are relics of the ancient festivals which celebrated the coming of spring at the disappearance of the **Pleiades** in April, and their rising again in May.

The Queen of the May is the ancient mother Amba, the chief star of the **Pleiades**, who was, according to Indian tradition, the promised bride of the King of Saubha, the city of the magicians, and, therefore, the wonder-working mother Maga *[D.F.A.'s note: Very similar to the Pleiades' star name Maia]*, who, from the apparently lifeless egg of the clouds and revolving moon, which bring the April showers, has created the living life of summer, and who has given her name to the month of May.

Also, the Maypole is the Tur, the sacred house and meridian pole, the god of the Tur-vasu, whose god, the Tur, was the heavenly fire-drill, which carried the stars round with him in his revolutions.

<u>These people began their year in April with the disappearance of the **Pleiades** below the horizon at sunset, the time when the worlds egg, the Easter eggs, were laid</u>, and when the Northern moon-hare, the Easter-hare of Southern Europe, started on her annual series of monthly races as the crescent moon, which, after becoming full, returns again to its original form ; the home earth to which the Indian fox, who was, as I have shown above, the original moon-hare, always comes back when hunted.

...

R. G. Haliburton offered additional Maypole/Pleiades connections in his paper, Notes on Mount Atlas and its traditions:

"The Susis have a May day festival at which the 'pole of Maia' is set up, at the summit of which is a doll composed of heads of wheat.

"Saints climb up the tree and scatter the wheat among the people, calling it 'our life,' 'our sustenance.'

"The Mexicans used to erect an enormous cross, the symbol of rain, and on its summit was placed a similar doll, which when reached by those climbing the pole, was scattered among the people, who treasured the fragments as something sacred, while the deity represented was called 'our life,' 'our support.'

"The coincidence is certainly very remarkable, for precisely the same words were addressed by the Iroquois to the three beneficent maidens residing in the **Pleiades**, who brought each her gift to mortals, the maize, the squash, and the bean. "

Similarly, Haliburton later says:

"The people of Sus also believe that there is a certain night in the year when the stars hold a solemn festival, in which all the angels and the spirits of the great kings of old take part.

"The very words of the song of the Pleiades, who are known in the New World as well as in the Old, as ' the dancers,' 'the Celestial chorus' of the Greeks, 'the Heavenly Host' of the Hebrews, and 'the seven dancers' of the North American Indians, are familiar to ears that can catch 'the music of the spheres,' and have been repeated to me by one of those favored mortals, a Susi wanderer from the Sahara: 'Oh Moon, oh Mother, we hold our feast to-night, We are dancing before God, between heaven and earth,' ...words that recall Milton's allusion to those 'morning stars that sang together with joy' at the creation, 'And the Pleiades before him danced, Shedding sweet influences.'

"This celestial festival evidently takes place on that night in November, when the full moon and the Pleiades are on the meridian together, for there is a Susi love song, 'Oh come to me my love, and long remain, For the Pleiades are meeting the moon to-night.'

"On that very night in November some tribes of the Australians still celebrate 'the sweet influences of the Pleiades,' and hold a grand corroboree in their honor, for ' they are the children of the Sun and Moon,' and 'are very good to the blackfellows.' " (1883)

Throughout these references, we see words and concepts consistent with Celtic beliefs and practices in Ireland, England, Scotland and through the British realm.

In addition, the traditions of the Tuatha De Danann of Ireland -- the "gods and not-gods " of pre-Milesian times -- fit the descriptions of the Pleiadians. They're generally described as very tall and fair, with a height of eight feet or -- in some cases, such as the Dagda -- giants.

The Dagda is a father-figure (he is also known as Eochaid Ollathair, or "All-father ") and a protector of the tribe.

In some accounts, the Tuatha De Danann arrived in Ireland "from the north. " Some interpret that as a reference to the arrival of the Norse. Others believe that it's describing ships that arrived from the sky.

From the *Dictionary of Greek and Roman antiquities,* by Sir William Smith:

Certain remarkable appearances fixed upon at a very early period to mark the approach of summer and winter, such as the rising and setting of the **Pleiades,** may have by custom or tradition become so completely identified in the minds of the people with particular days, that the compilers of calendars intended for general use, while they desired to register accurate observations, were compelled at the same time to include those which, belonging to remote ages and foreign lands, had nevertheless acquired a prescriptive claim to attention.

We begin with the most important, — the **Pleiades**, Arctums, and Sirius, which we shall discuss fully, and then add a few words upon others of less note.

### THE PLEIADES.

HESIOD. — Hesiod indicates the period of harvest by the rising of the Atlas-born Pleiads *(Erg.* 384) after they had remained concealed for forty days and forty nights.

Now in the age of Hesiod (a. c. 800), the heliacal rising of the Pleiads took place at Athens, according to the computation of Ideler, on the 19th of May of the Julian Calendar, which is just the season when the wheat crop comes to maturity in that climate.

Again, he indicates the commencement of the ploughing season, and the close of the season for navigating, by the morning setting of the Pleiads, which in that age and latitude fell about the third of the Julian November.

Varro, where he describes the distribution of the year into eight divisions, according to the calendar of Caesar, states that there was a space of forty-six days from the vernal equinox (25th March) to the rising of the Pleiades ( *Vergiliarum exortum),* which is thus fixed to the 8th or 9th of May. *(R. R.* i.28.)

(2.) Pliny (xviii. 66. § 1) names the 10th of May.

Columella has three distinct notices [including the 22nd of April, the 7th of May, and the 10th of May] ; this last corresponds with his assertion elsewhere, that the phenomenon takes place forty-eight days after the vernal equinox (ix. 14. § 4).

Now the true morning rising of the Pleiads took place at Rome in the age of the above writers, who arc all embraced within the limits of a century, about the 16th of April, the apparent or heliacal rising about the 28th of May.

Hence, not one of the above statements is accurate. But most approach closely to the observation of Euctemon (D. c. 430), according to whom the Pleiad rises on the 13th of Taurus (8th of May),  which expressly refers to the true rising, although inapplicable to Rome, will suit the latitude of Athens for the epoch in question.

Varro places the setting of the Pleiades (*Vergiliarum occasum*) forty-five days after the autumnal equinox (24th Sept.), that is, on the 6th or 7th of November *(R. R.* i. 28).

(2.) Pliny names the 11th of November (xviii. 60, 74 ; the text in c 59 is corrupt).

Columella, as before, has a succession of notices: 20th and 21st Oct., 28th Oct., 8th Nov., and 10th Nov. These are all taken from his calendar.

Now the true morning setting of the Pleiads took place for Rome at that epoch on the 29th of October, the apparent morning setting on the 9th of November.

The evening setting of the Pleiades took place, according to Columella, on the 6th of April; according to the calendar of Caesar on the 5th. These statements are not far from the truth, since the apparent evening setting took place at Rome for the Julian epoch on the 8th of April. The apparent evening rising belonged to the 25th of September.

VIRGIL. — Virgil *(Georg.* i. 221) enjoins the husbandman not to sow his wheat until after the morning setting of the **Pleiades.**

Hesiod, as we have seen above, fixes the commencement of the ploughing season, without making any distinction as to the particular crop desired, by the (apparent) morning setting of the **Pleiades**, that is, for his age, the beginning of November.

There is another passage where both the rising and the setting of the Pleiades are mentioned in connection with the two periods of the honey harvest.

Here, again, there is nothing in the context by which we can ascertain the precise periods which the poet desired to define, we can only make a guess by comparing his injunction with those of others. Columella (xi. 2) recommends that the combs should be cut, *if full,* about the 22nd of April; but, since he adds that if they are not full the operation ought to be deferred, the matter is left quite indefinite.

In like manner the last-named writer advises (xi. 2. § 57) that the autumnal collection of honey should be put off until the month of October, although others were in the habit of beginning earlier. The true morning setting was, as already stated, on the 28th of October, the apparent on the 9th of November.

According to Ovid, *Pleiades incipiunt humerog relevare paternos Quae septem dici, sex tamen esse solent.*

That is, the Pleiades were the daughters of Atlas, who supported the heavens on hit shoulders, and hence, when they disappeared from the sky, they might be said to remove a portion of their father's burden *humeros relevare paternos.*

Again, the Pleiades are said to rise visibly in the morning on May 14 th, marking the end of spring and the beginning of summer. Now the heliacal rising of the Pleiades did not take place at Rome when Ovid wrote until May 28th ; but the phenomenon in question took place at Athens on May 16th in the age of Melon.

<u>Hence this observation was evidently copied from a Greek calendar computed for the fifth century B. C.</u>

VIRGIL, HORACE. — Both Virgil and Horace frequently allude to the tempests which accompanied the winter setting of Orion, just as Hesiod *(Erg.* 617) eight hundred years before had warned the mariner that when the **Pleiades,** fleeing from the might of Orion, plunge into the dark main :

The apparent morning Setting of Orion, which in the time of Hesiod commenced early in November, soon after the morning setting of the **Pleiades,** thus became connected in traditional lore with the first gales of the rainy season. The association continued for centuries, although the phenomenon itself became gradually further and further removed from the beginning of the stormy period.

In the Parapegma of Geminus we find notices by three different astronomers, in which the setting of the **Pleiades** and of Orion are mentioned as attended by tempests, although each of the three fixes upon a different day.

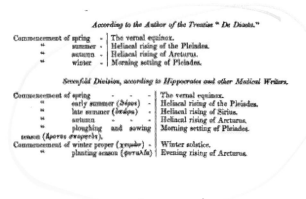

In reviewing this literature, we see the dramatic significance of the Pleiades in the daily lives and spiritual beliefs of cultures around the world.

Those beliefs and practices were so significant, they remained embedded in more modern routines and religions, albeit somewhat disguised.

The importance of this cannot be missed: There are other constellations they could have used for their calendars, including Taurus.

Somewhere in this mix of fact and folklore, there is an extraordinary emphasis on the Pleiades. If they're "just stars, " why would this happen across so many cultures?

Perhaps the gods who became or originated in the Pleiades are the same Pleiadians we study today. In history and pre-history, they simply became part of an oral tradition that preserved the core importance of these entities.

## The Pleiades in the Bible

The Pleiades is mentioned at least three times in the
Bible. The following is an annotated excerpt from
Smith's Bible Dictionary. I've added paragraph breaks
for modern readers, and placed the words 'Pleiades' in
bold type when you might want to skim the reference
rather than read it, line-by-line.

I've also added the *actual* Bible references from the
King James Version. All mid-quote additions are in a
modern font.

Also, I've underlined a few important phrases from
Smith's discussion of this. (Remember, this is quoted
from the expanded, *original* version of Smith's book,
not the abbreviated later edition.)

It's important to consider the possibility -- albeit it
somewhat heretical to some -- that there were
confusions between the acts of God and those of
enlightened and advanced beings, including the
Pleiadeans.

In some cases, reading between the lines, you may see
references to truth as 'light' and additional phrases that
could suggest telepathic communication and 'invisible'
forms of contact.

For that reason, I've included the *full* Bible passages,
outlining the might, abilities and influences of the
entity (or entities) that may be involved.

Read them carefully. Clues are there.

*This begins the excerpt from Smith's Bible Dictionary.*

**Pleiades** - The Hebrew word (cimah) so rendered
occurs in Job 9:9; 38:31; Amos 6:8 In the last passage

our Authorized Version has 'the seven stars,' although the Geneva version translates the word 'Pleiades' as in the other cases. The Pleiades are a group of stars situated on the shoulder of the constellation Taurus.

¹ Then Job answered and said, ² I know *it is* so of a truth: but how should man be just with God? ³ If he will contend with him, he cannot answer him one of a thousand. ⁴ *He is* wise in heart, and mighty in strength: who hath hardened *himself* against him, and hath prospered? ⁵ Which removeth the mountains, and they know not: which overturneth them in his anger. ⁶ Which shaketh the earth out of her place, and the pillars thereof tremble. ⁷ Which commandeth the sun, and it riseth not; and sealeth up the stars. ⁸ Which alone spreadeth out the heavens, and treadeth upon the waves of the sea. ⁹ Which maketh Arcturus, Orion, and **Pleiades**, and the chambers of the south. ¹⁰ Which doeth great things past finding out; yea, and wonders without number. ¹¹ <u>Lo, he goeth by me, and I see *him* not: he passeth on also, but I perceive him not</u>.

Job 9:1-11 (KJV)

In Job, the LXX. has [a symbol], the order of the Hebrew words having been altered, while in Amos there is no trace of the original, and it is difficult to imagine what the translators had before them.

Note: In other words, these passages started as oral traditions and were successively changed as they were written down, then translated, and sometimes translated again.

For this reason -- with all due respect for those who believe that the Bible is literally true, inerrant, and complete -- we need to be flexible in our interpretation of some of these passages.

## Chapter 38

1 Then the Lord answered Job out of the whirlwind, and said, 2 Who is this that darkeneth counsel by words without knowledge? 3 Gird up now thy loins like a man; for I will demand of thee, and answer thou me.

4 Where wast thou when I laid the foundations of the earth? declare, if thou hast understanding. 5 Who hath laid the measures thereof, if thou knowest? or who hath stretched the line upon it? 6 Whereupon are the foundations thereof fastened? or who laid the corner stone thereof; 7 <u>When the morning stars sang together</u>, and all the sons of God shouted for joy? 8 Or who shut up the sea with doors, when it brake forth, as if it had issued out of the womb? 9 When I made the cloud the garment thereof, and thick darkness a swaddlingband for it, 10 And brake up for it my decreed place, and set bars and doors, 11 And said, Hitherto shalt thou come, but no further: and here shall thy proud waves be stayed?

12 Hast thou commanded the morning since thy days; and caused the dayspring to know his place; 13 That it might take hold of the ends of the earth, that the wicked might be shaken out of it? 14 It is turned as clay to the seal; and they stand as a garment. 15 <u>And from the wicked their light is withholden</u>, and the high arm shall be broken.

16 Hast thou entered into the springs of the sea? or hast thou walked in the search of the depth?

17 Have the gates of death been opened unto thee? or hast thou seen the doors of the shadow of death? 18 Hast thou perceived the breadth of the earth? declare if thou knowest it all.

19 <u>Where is the way where light dwelleth?</u> and as for darkness, where is the place thereof, 20 That thou shouldest take it to the bound thereof, and that thou shouldest know the paths to the house thereof? 21 Knowest thou it, because thou wast then born? or because the number of thy days is great?

22 Hast thou entered into the treasures of the snow? or hast thou seen the treasures of the hail, 23 Which I have reserved against the time of trouble, against the day of battle and war?

24 By what way is the light parted, which scattereth the east wind upon the earth?

25 Who hath divided a watercourse for the overflowing of waters, or a way for the lightning of thunder; 26 To cause it to rain on the earth, where no man is; on the wilderness, wherein there is no man; 27 To satisfy the desolate and waste ground; and to cause the bud of the tender herb to spring forth? 28 Hath the rain a father? or who hath begotten the drops of dew? 29 Out of whose womb came the ice? and the hoary frost of heaven, who hath gendered it? 30 The waters are hid as with a stone, and the face of the deep is frozen.

31 <u>Canst thou bind the sweet influences of **Pleiades**, or loose the bands of Orion?</u>

32 Canst thou bring forth Mazzaroth in his season? or canst thou guide Arcturus with his sons?

33 Knowest thou the ordinances of heaven? canst thou set the dominion thereof in the earth? 34 Canst thou lift

up thy voice to the clouds, that abundance of waters may cover thee? 35 Canst thou send lightnings, that they may go, and say unto thee, Here we are?

36 <u>Who hath put wisdom in the inward parts? or who hath given understanding to the heart?</u> 37 Who can number the clouds in wisdom? or who can stay the bottles of heaven, 38 When the dust groweth into hardness, and the clods cleave fast together? 39 Wilt thou hunt the prey for the lion? or fill the appetite of the young lions, 40 When they couch in their dens, and abide in the covert to lie in wait? 41 Who provideth for the raven his food? when his young ones cry unto God, they wander for lack of meat.

Job 38:1-41 (KJV)

The Vulgate in each passage has a different rendering :
*Hijiules* iii Job ix. 9.

Note: My modern-day copy of the Vulgate says the following. *What has been changed, when, <u>and why</u>?*

…qui facit <u>Arcturum</u> et Oriona et Hyadas et interiora austri…

Job 9:9 (Vulgate)

*Pleiades* in Job xxxviii. 31

…numquid coniungere valebis micantes stellas **Pliadis** aut gyrum Arcturi poteris dissipare…

Job 38:31 (Vulgate)

*Arcturus* in Am. v. 8.

8 Seek him that maketh **the seven stars** and Orion, and turneth the shadow of death into the morning, and maketh the day dark with night: that calleth for the waters of the sea, and poureth them out upon the face of the earth: The Lord is his name…

Amos 5:8 (KJV)

…facientem <u>Arcturum</u> et Orionem et convertentem in mane tenebras et diem nocte mutantem qui vocat aquas maris et effundit eas super faciem terrae Dominus nomen eius

Amos 5:8 (Vulgate)

Some Jewish commentators are no less at variance.

R. David Kimchi in his Lexicon says, ' R. Jonah wrote that it was a collection of stars called in Arabic *Al Thuraiya.'* That *Thuraiya* and the Pleiades are the same is proved by the words of Aben Ragel. '*Al Thuraiya* is the mansion of the moon, in the sign Taurus, and it is called the celestial hen with her chickens.'

With this, Hyde compares the Fr. *pulsiniere,* and Eng. *hen and chickens,* which are old names for the same stars.

The opinion of Aben Ezra has been frequently misrepresented. He held that *Cimah* was a single large star, *Aldebaran,* the brightest of the Hyades, while *Cesil* [A. V. ' Orion '] was *Antares,* the heart of Scorpio.

On the whole, though it is impossible to arrive at any certain conclusion, it appears that our translators were perfectly justified in rendering *Cimah* by 'Pleiades.'

Hea, or Hoa, the third god of the Assyrian triad, was known among the stars by the name of Kimmut, which Rawlinson compares with the Heb. *Cimah,* and identifies wilh the constellation Draco.

*Note:* In later editions of Smith's Bible Dictionary, everything above -- after the Job 9:11 quotation -- was reduced to these two sentences:

> The rendering 'sweet influences' of the Authorized Version, Job 38:31 is a relic of the lingering belief in the power which the stars exerted over human destiny. But Schaff thinks the phrase arose from the fact that the Pleiades appear about the middle of April, and hence are associated with the return of spring, the season of sweet influences.

Likewise, in the modern *King James Bible Dictionary,* the only Bible reference under the entry for Pleiades is Job 8:8-9. The Bible's *other* references to Pleiades are omitted altogether.

And in the Schaff-Herzog encyclopedia of religious knowledge, the lengthy passages about the Pleiades appear *only in the 1911 edition.*

Why would they do that? *What are they trying to hide?*

Much seems to weigh upon the interpretation of the word *kesil*.

Under the entry for Orion, *Easton's Illustrated Dictionary* says:

Orion

Heb. Kesil; i.e., 'the fool', the name of a constellation (Job 9:9; Job 38:31; Amos 5:8) consisting of about eighty stars. The Vulgate renders thus, but the LXX. renders by Hesperus, i.e., 'the evening-star,' Venus. The Orientals 'appear to have conceived of this constellation under the figure of an impious giant bound upon the sky.' This giant was, according to tradition, Nimrod, the type of the folly that contends against God. In Isa 13:10 the plural form of the Hebrew word is rendered 'constellations.'

Reviewing the Bible's references to the stars, and passages that may be relevant to our understanding of the Pleiades as well as the Pleiadians, we need to include a few traditional and modern notes about the Bible and related resources.

For example, Easton's Illustrated Dictionary says this about Arcturus:

"Bear-keeper, the name given by the ancients to the brightest star in the constellation Bootes. In the Authorized Version (Job 9:9; Job 38:32) it is the rendering of the Hebrew word 'ash, which probably designates the constellation the Great Bear. This word ('ash) is supposed to be derived from an Arabic word meaning <u>night-watcher</u>, because the Great Bear always revolves about the pole, and to our nothern hemisphere never sets. "

Is it possible that 'night watcher' references the vigilant and watchful presence of the Pleiadians, filtered through the context and mythology of early astronomical studies?

Is this also a reference to the Watchers in Enoch?

By understanding the context of early Hebrew beliefs, we may find insights separating spiritual, Scriptural and scientific truths, *and* showing how they overlapped in the minds of early scholars.

In Easton's entry for astronomy, we read this:

"'The Hebrews were devout students of the wonders of the starry firmanent (Amos 5:8; Ps 19).

"In the Book of Job, which is the oldest book of the Bible in all probability, the constellations are distinguished and named. Mention is made of the 'morning star' (Rev 2:28; Compare Isa 14:12), the 'seven stars' and '**Pleiades**,' 'Orion,' 'Arcturus,' the 'Great Bear' (Amos 5:8; Job 9:9; Job 38:31), 'the crooked serpent,' Draco (Job 26:13), the Dioscuri, or Gemini, 'Castor and Pollux' (Acts 28:11). <u>The stars were called 'the host of heaven'</u> (Isa 40:26; Jer 33:22).

"The oldest divisions of time were mainly based on the observation of the movements of the heavenly bodies, the 'ordinances of heaven' (Gen 1:14-18; Job 38:33; Jer 31:35; Jer 33:25). Such observations led to the division of the year into months and the mapping out of the appearances of the stars into twelve portions, which received from the Greeks the name of the 'zodiac.'

'"The word 'Mazzaroth' (Job 38:32) means, as the margin notes, 'the twelve signs' of the zodiac. 'Astronomical observations were also necessary among the Jews in order to the fixing of the proper time for sacred ceremonies, the 'new moons,' the 'passover,' etc.

"Many allusions are found to the display of God's wisdom and power as seen in the starry heavens (Ps 8; Ps 19:1-6; Isa 51:6) "

*Hitchcock's Dictionary of Bible Names* translates 'Arcturus' as simply 'a gathering together.'

Interestingly, the word 'religion' comes from *re* (to return, to renew, to revisit) and *ligare* (to gather or bind together).

At least semantically, that suggests a connection between spirituality and this study of the Pleiades.

Edited and annotated from *The new Schaff-Herzog encyclopedia of religious knowledge (1911)*

"Fixed stars appear to be mentioned in:

- Amos v. 8 (the Pleiades);
- Isa. xiii. 10, where the English ' constellations ' adequately represents the Hebrew ' Orions '

From the Vulgate:

...quoniam stellae caeli et splendor earum non expandent lumen suum obtenebratus est sol in ortu suo et luna non splendebit in lumine suo

Isaiah 13:10 (Vulgate)

From the King James Version:

For the stars of heaven and the <u>constellations</u>
thereof shall not give their light: the sun shall be
darkened in his going forth, and the moon shall not
cause her light to shine.

Isaiah 13:10 (KJV)

- Job ix. 9, the Bear or Arcturus, Orion, the
  Pleiades, and ' the chambers of the south '
- Job xxxviii. 31-32, the Pleiades, Orion, the signs
  of the Zodiac, and Arcturus or the Bear.

"Two pairs of Hebrew words occur, *kesil* and *kimah,* of
which the first probably is Orion and the second the
Pleiades; to Constellations.

"This as the meaning of *kesil* the Septuagint testifies, as
well as the Syriac and the Targum.

"The Hebrews saw in the constellation of Orion a
human form, a giant chained to the heavens, and post-
Biblical tradition called him Nimrod.

"The Septuagint also testifies to the **Pleiades** as the
rendering of *kimah.*

"Bar Ah (Gesenius, Thesaurus, p. 665) confirms this,
though he points out other meanings for the word and
many Syrians understood by it Arcturus.

"The Talmud's use shows that *kimah* is not to be
understood of a single star (cf. Job xxxviii. 31), and the
conception seems frequent that the **Pleiades** were
bound together by bonds, and were spoken of as a

rosette or a nosegay, while the Talmud (in Berachoth 58b) speaks of the **Pleiades** as of 100 stars.

"Stern has supposed that *kimah* is Sirius, i.e., that the stars of Job ix. 9 are all in the same declination of the heavens.

"In that case, since *kesil* is surely Orion, the other names in the passage designate Sirius, the Hyades, and the Pleiades.

"Hoffmann, who in general agrees with Stern, then makes the ' sweet influences' (Job xxxviii. 31) refer to the overflow of the Nile, preceded by the early rising of Sirius.

"But this must be rejected as impossible; no Hebrew could have understood ' canst thou bind the refreshings of Sirius? '

"This and like interpretations are shattered on the imperative conclusion that *kimah* must mean a group of stars.

"The Arabic equivalent of this word means ' heaps '; the Assyrian cognate *kimtu* is used for ' family.' "

Later, in that same book, it says:

"The ' chambers of the south ' of Job ix. 9 is probably to be explained by the many bright stars in Argo, the Cross, and the Centaur visible on the southern horizon in the regal period of Hebrew history, out of which, however, definite figures had not been made.

"The Hebrew *mazzaroth* of Job xxxviii. 32 is probably a scribal error for the *mazzaloth* of II Kings xxiii. 5, though it may represent a different pronunciation of the same word. It is of Assyrian origin, and denotes ' position,' i.e., of <u>astral deities,</u> <u>and then the deities themselves.</u> '"

That last note will be important when we talk about the Pleiades and beliefs of the Jehovah's Witnesses.

**The Pleiades and Theosophy**

In Theosophy, it is believed the Seven Stars of the **Pleiades** focus the spiritual energy of the Seven Rays from the Galactic Logos to the Seven Stars of the Great Bear. From there, the energy is transmitted to Sirius, then to the Sun, then to the god of Earth (Sanat Kumara) and finally through the seven Masters of the Seven Rays to us.

According to Theosophical teachings from 1919, the number seven is closely connected with the occult significance of the **Pleiades**, referencing those seven daughters of Atlas, 'the six present, the seventh hidden.'

In Theosophy, the Pleiades also have a close connection with continent of Atlantis.

...

The following is from *Theosophy,* volume 11, published in April 1896:

"The sun, it is known now by astronomers, as it was known by the ancients (who were ourselves in fact), revolves around a centre. That is, that while we are going around the sun, he is going around some other centre, so that we describe in the sky not a circle around the sun, but a spiral, as we move with the sun around his enormous orbit.

"Now do you grasp that idea exactly ? It is a very important one, for it opens up the subject to a very large extent. There is a star somewhere in the sky, we do not know where—some think it is Alcyone, or some other star, some think it may be a star in the **Pleiades**, and some others think it is a star somewhere else—but they know by deduction from the known to the unknown, that the sun is attracted himself by some unknown centre, and that he turns around it in an enormous circle, and as he turns, of course he draws the earth with him. "

...

I have already mentioned a connection between the Pleiades, the Pleiadians, and Atlantis.

In the *Theosophical Glossary,* Mme. Blavatsky said:

"Atlantidae (Gr.). - The ancestors of the Pharaohs and the forefathers of the Egyptians, according to some, and as the Esoteric Science teaches. (See Sec. Doct., Vol. II., and Esoteric Buddhism.)

"Plato heard of this highly civilized people, the last remnant of which was submerged 9,000 years before his day, from Solon, who had it from the High Priests of Egypt.

"Voltaire, the eternal scoffer, was right in stating that the Atlantidae (our fourth Root Race) made their appearance in Egypt.

"It was in Syria and in Phrygia, as well as Egypt, that they established the worship of the Sun.

"Occult philosophy teaches that the Egyptians were a remnant of the last Aryan Atlantidae. "

Reading between the lines, it appears that some believe that Atlantis was connected to the Pleiades, and that the Atlanteans came from Pleiades (and were Pleiadians) and/or left for the Pleiades (and are now Pleiadians) when Atlantis was facing destruction.

However, some of the Atlanteans may have chosen Egypt as their home, either before, during or after their civilization (and perhaps they, as well) lived in the Pleiades and became known as Pleiadians.

We've already seen some evidence of a Pleiadian connection with the early Egyptians.  In some of the next several observations -- related to Theosophy -- this may be confirmed.

The following passages are from the *Theosophical Outlook,* published in December 1919.

THE PLEIADES. (From the "Secret Doctrine. ")

It (Virgo) is inseparable from Leo, the sign that precedes it, and from the **Pleiades** and their sisters, the Hyades, of which Aldebaran is the brilliant leader.

All these are connected with the periodical renovations of the Earth, with regard to its continents—even Ganymedes, who in astronomy is Aquarius.—Vol. II, 829.

The Greek allegories give to Atlas, or <u>Atlantis</u>, seven daughters—seven subraces—whose respective names are Maia, Electra, Taygeta, Asterope, Merope, Alcyone, and Ccloeno.
        *Celseno*

This ethnologically — as they are credited with having married Gods and with having become the mothers of famous heroes, the founders of many nations and cities.

Astronomically, the Atlantides have become the seven **Pleiades** (?).

In Occult Science the two are connected with the destinies of nations, those destinies being shaped by the past events of their early lives according to Karmic law.—Vol. II, 81I.

The famous Orphic Hymn on the great periodical cataclysm divulges the whole Esotericism of the event.

Pluto, in the Pit, carries off Eurydice, bitten by the Polar Serpent. Then Leo, the Lion, is vanquished. Now when the Lion is "in the Pit, " or below the South Pole, then Virgo, as the next sign, follows him, and when her head, down to the waist, is below the southern horizon—she is inverted.

On the other hand, the Hyades are the rain or Deluge constellations; and Aldebaran—he who follows or succeeds the daughters of Atlas, or the **Pleiades**— looks down from the eye of Taurus. It is from this point of the ecliptic that the calculations of the new cycle were commenced.—Vol. II. 830.

The **Pleiades** (Alcyone, especially) are thus considered even in Astronomy, as the central point around which our universe of fixed stars revolves, the focus from which, and into which, the Divine Breath, Motion, works incessantly during the Manvantara.—Vol. II, 582.

"At the time when the summer tropical 'colure' passed through the Pleiades, when Cor Leonis would be upon the Equator, and when Leo was vertical to Ceylon at sunset, then would Taurus be vertical to the island of Atlantis at noon. "—Vol. II. 426.

Niobe ... is the daughter of one of the **Pleiades**, or
Atlantides, the granddaughter of Atlas, therefore,
because she represents the last generations of the
doomed Continent (Atlantis).—Vol. II, 815.

Number Seven is closely connected with the occult
significance of the Pleiades, those seven daughters of
Atlas, "the six present, the seventh hidden.'

In India they are connected with their nursling, the war
God, Karttikeya.

It was the **Pleiades** (in Sanskrit, Krittakas) who gave
this name to the God Karttikeya being the planet Mars,
astronomically. As a God he is the son of Rudra, born
without the intervention of a woman. He is a Kumara, a
"virgin youth " again, generated in the fire from the
Seed of Shiva—the Holy Spirit— hence called Agni-
Ghu.

The late Dr. Kenealy believed that, in India, Karttikeya
is the secret symbol of the Cycle of the Naros,
composed of 600, 666, and 777 years, according to
whether solar or lunar, divine or mortal, years are
counted; and that the six visible, or the seven actual
sisters, the **Pleiades**, areneeded for the completion of
this most secret and mysterious of all the astronomical
and religious symbols. Therefore, when intended to
commemorate one particular event, Karttikeya was
shown, of old, as a Kumara, as Ascetic, with six heads—
one for each century of the Naros.

When the symbolism was needed for another event,
then, in conjunction with the seven sidereal sisters,
Kartitikeya is seen accompanied by Kaumari, or Sena,
his female aspect.—I'ol. II, 654.

Meanwhile it is the Seven Rishis (Great Bear) who
mark the time and duration of events in our septenary

Lifecycle. They are as mysterious as their supposed wives, the **Pleiades**, of whom only one—she who hides—has proven virtuous.

The **Pleiades**, or Krittikas, are the nurses of Karttikeya, the God of War (the Mars of the Western Pagans) who is called the Commander of the Celestial Armies, or rather of the Siddhas— Siddha-sena (translated Yogis in Heaven, and holy Sages on the Earth)—which would make Karttikeya identical with Michael, the "Leader of the Celestial Hosts, " and, like himself, a virgin Kumara. Verily he is the Guha, the "Mysterious One, " as much so as are the Saptarshis and the Krittikas.

The seven Rishis and the Pleiades, for the interpretation of all these combined reveal to the Adept the greatest mysteries of Occult Nature. —Vol. II, 579.

When Karttikeya was delivered to the Krititka by the Gods to be nursed, they were only six, whence Karttikeya is represented with six heads; but when the poetical fancy of the early Aryan symbologists made of them the consorts of the seven Rishis, they were seven. . . . Anyhow, the seven Rishis were made to marry the seven Krittika before the disappearance of the seventh Pleiad.—Vol. II, 581. .

*From that same publication:*

## A Theosophical comment on astrology and the Pleiades

There must be something wrong in a system that combines the influences of the planets, which are definite bodies moving in space, and the influence of arbitrary divisions of space irrespective of the stars that they contain, while wholly disregarding the stars that were once contained in those spaces, but that are there no longer.

The astrologer is led into further inconsistencies when he attributes influences to certain of the fixed stars, as most good astrologers do.

Alcyone, for example, is a star of the **Pleiades**, and the Pleiades are in Taurus. But when the astrologer is considering the influence of Alcyone he must lift it bodily away from Taurus and put it in some other "Sign, " inasmuch as the constellation of Taurus is nowhere near the place at which he has marked it on his nativity.

He must be guilty of the almost incredible heresy of saying that Alcyone is not in Taurus at all, but in some other "Sign, " whereas Alcyone cannot be anywhere else but in Taurus.

The Hindu astrology is not so inconsistent as this. It deals with the groups of stars that make up the Zodiac, and not with the arbitrary divisions of space that once contained those stars.

*From the same publication in July 1919:*

On a possible planet of Alpha Centauri the inhabitants would be seeing the earthly events of 1915, <u>while an inhabitant of a possible **Pleiades** system would see the inhabitants of the earth making history as far back as about 1200.</u>

Some planetarian out in space may be at this moment watching the arrival of William the Conqueror in England, and another somewhere may even he seeing the Missing Link roaming the earth.

It is merely a question of sufficiently sensitive instruments, for a continuous reel of pictures leaves the earth and travels through space, suffering only a diminution of brightness.

*From The Theosophical Glossary,* "Pillaloo Codi *(Tamil).* A nickname in popular astronomy given to the **Pleiades**, meaning "hen and chickens ". The French also, curiously enough call this constellation, " Poussiniere. "

In *Earth's earliest ages, and their connection with modern spiritualism and theosophy,* George Hawkins Pember wrote:

For in 1748 the astronomer Bradley gave a hint, which others have subsequently developed and confirmed, that our solar system, together with the whole of the sidereal heavens within range of our vision and telescopes, is but a portion of an inconceivably vast circle of stars revolving around one centre. <u>And that centre, the pivot of the universe, is now supposed to be among the Pleiades.</u>

If this be the case, wonderful indeed are " the' sweet influences of Pleiades " which keep the whole of the starry heavens in orderly motion.

...

These beliefs are echoed in this passage from *Theosophical Siftings:*

Taurus, or the Bull, is the second sign, and is made by
Subba Row to correspond with the Hindu sacred word
*num*. *The Secret Doctrine* tells us that this sign was
sacred in every cosmogony, with the Hindus as with the
Zoroastrians, with the Chaldees as with the Egyptians.
In *Isis Unveiled* we are toid that Taurus is the symbol
of the Satya Yuga, the Golden Age, and if we calculate
the position of the vernal equinox for the conclusion of
the Kali Yuga or Black Age, and the dawn of the Satya
or Golden Age, we find that it *will* coincide with
*Taurus*.

I need not remind you that the constellation Taurus
includes the group of stars known as the **Pleiades**, of
which Alcyone is the chief. It will also be known to you
that, according to some recent scientific theories, our
sun is travelling around a centre of his own, which
centre is Alcyone. Maedler calculates the length of his
circuit around Alcyone to be 180,000,000 years.

Taurus I take to be spiritual, male creative force on the
highest plane. Male creative force on all the planes. In
Egyptian cosmogony Taurus corresponds to Osiris in
his four aspects—Osiris Ptah, the spiritual aspect;
Osiris Horus, the intellectual inanasic aspect; Osiris
Lunus, the lunar, psychic, astral aspect; and Osiris
Typhon, the material, passionate, turbulent nature.
Taurus is perhaps the Hindu Daksha who, we are told,
is:—

   "The spiritual power, and at the same time the male
energy that generates the Gods in eternity. The
generative force, spiritual at the commencement,
becomes at the most material end of its evolution a
procreative force on the physical plane. "

Taurus is symbolized by the Tribe of Issachar, because
he is "a strong ass couching down. "

...

In a similar vein,  S. H. Keir Moilliet said in *Broad Lines; or the true theosophy:*

The pyramid is supposed to be a symbol of the world, which the ancients considered to be a plane circle, not a spheroid.

That figure is exactly represented by a pyramid, the base of which is, as we have seen, a plane circle squared.

It has been noticed in Job xxxviii. 4, 5, 6, allusion is made to the foundations of the earth, the measures, the line, the corner-stone thereof, as if it were a vast pyramid.

The sunken sockets found in the levelled rock, into which the inferior corner-stones of the Great Pyramid have been carefully fitted, is thought to bear reference to the creation of the world.

The words, ' When the morning stars sang together,' etc., and ' Canst thou bind the sweet influences of the **Pleiades**,' etc., <u>may allude to the date when the present astronomical cycle began</u>.

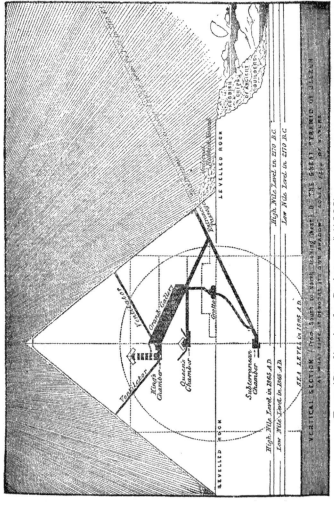

From "Studies in the Scriptures" (1908)

In *Studies in the Scriptures,* part of the Watch Tower series in the book, *Thy Kingdom Come* (Millenial Dawn, Vol. III), we see further illumination about the Pleiades-pyramid connection.

Though this information was interpreted in contrast with many Theosophical beliefs, it's included here because the *pyramid* information is relevant in this context.

"Prof. Smyth has concluded that the Great Pyramid was builded in the year 2170 B. C, reaching this conclusion, first, from astronomical observations. Perceiving that the upward passage angles correspond to a telescope, and that the " Entrance Passage" corresponds to an astronomer's "pointer, " he set about to investigate to what particular star it could have pointed at any time in the past.

"Calculations showed that a Draconis, the dragon-star, had occupied a position in the heavens which looked directly down the entrance, at midnight of the autumnal equinox, B. C 2170.

"Then, considering himself as an astronomer at that date, with his pointer fixed upon a Draconis, and considering the ascending passages as though they were a telescope, which they much resemble, he calculated what constellation or what notable star would have been before his telescope thus fixed at the particular date indicated by his pointer, and found that it must have been the **Pleiades**.

"So wonderful a coincidence convinced him that the date of the Great Pyramid's building was thus indicated; for a Draconis is no less a symbol of sin and Satan than **Pleiades** is a symbol of God and the center of the universe. "

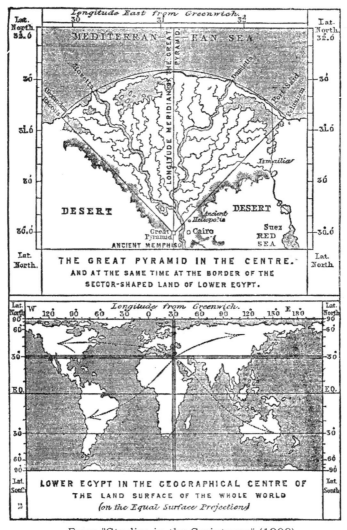

From "Studies in the Scriptures" (1908)

"Commenting upon the scientific testimony and the location of this majestic "Witness, " Rev. Joseph Seiss, D. D. suggests:

"There is a yet grander thought embodied in this wonderful structure.

Of its five points there is one of special pre-eminence, in which all its sides and exterior lines terminate. It is the summit corner, which lifts its solemn index finger to the sun at midday, and by its distance from the base tells the mean distance to that sun from the earth.

And if we go back to the date which the Pyramid gives itself, and look for what that finger pointed to at midnight, we find a far sublimer indication.

Science has at last discovered that the sun is not a dead center, with planets wheeling about it, but itself stationary.

It is now ascertained that the sun also is in motion, carrying with it its splendid retinue of comets, planets, its satellites and theirs, around some other and vastly mightier center.

Astronomers are not yet fully agreed as to what or where that center is. Some, however, believe that they have found the directon of it to be the Pleiades, and particularly Alcyone, the central one of the renowned Pleiadic stars.

To the distinguished German astronomer, Prof. J. H. Maedler, belongs the honor of having made this discovery.

Alcyone, then, as far as science has been able to perceive, would seem to be ' the midnight throne' in which the whole system of gravitation has its central

seat, and from which the Almighty governs his
universe.

And here is the wonderful corresponding fact, that at
the date of the Great Pyramid's building, at midnight of
the autumnal equinox, and hence the true beginning of
the year as still preserved in the traditions of many
nations, the **Pleiades** were distributed over the
meridian of this Pyramid, with Alcyone (rj Tauri ")
precisely on the line.

"Here, then, is a pointing of the highest and sublimest
character that mere human science has ever been able
so much as to hint, and which would seem to breathe
an unsuspected and mighty meaning into that speech
of God to Job, when he demanded, ' Canst thou bind
the sweet influences of Pleiades?'"

In *The theosophical forum*, a discussion of ancient and
modern physics includes an interesting note.  This is
the text from that journal:

The author of "Ancient and Modern Physics " suggests
that there are four kinds of substances connected with
our visible universe. The first and coarsest he calls
prakritic, taking the name from the Sanskrit word for
Nature.

The globe of the earth, including the atmosphere,
represents this prakritic substance, as do also the
globes of the other planets.

The solid earth is only nucleus of this prakritic globe,
and semi-gaseous planet like Jupiter and Saturn, some

ten times greater in diameter than the earth, are probably examples of the earth's earlier states.

The etheric substance comes next. The author of "Ancient and Modern Physics " conceives the Sun to be the nucleus of an immense etheric globe, which has, as it were, an etheric atmosphere stretching far beyond the limits of the solar system as we understand it, that is, beyond the orbit of the planet Neptune.

Then comes pranic substance, with the star Alcyone in the **Pleiades** as the center of an immense pranic globe, as much finer than the etheric globe as the latter is finer than gross matter.

Finally, we have manasic substance, which is the last and highest realm of the outer universe; all higher planes are subjective and spiritual.

The author of "Ancient and Modern Physics " conceives the visible universe to be a vast globe of manasic substance, infinitely more tenuous and subtle, infinitely more alive than the pranic globe already mentioned; and containing within it many pranic globes, just as the pranic globe of Alcyone contains within it many etheric sun-globes.

The number seven (7) keeps reappearing with references to the Pleiades. In a Theosophical journal, *Lucifer,* author said the following in *Numbers, the Occult Powers:*

THE HEPTAD. 7.

The Heptad say the followers of "Pythagoras, " was so called from the Greek verb "sebo, " to venerate (and from the Hebrew SʜBO, seven, or satisfied, abundance), being Septos "Holy, ""divine, " and "motherless, " and "a Virgin. "

From Nicomachus we learn that it was called "Minerva, " being unmarried and virginal, begotten neither by a mother, *i.e.* even number, nor from a father, *i.e.* odd number: but proceeding from the summit of the Father of all things, the Monad ; even as Minerva sprang all armed from the Forehead of Jove or Zeus.

Hence also Obrimopatre, or daughter of a mighty father, and Glaucopis, shining eyed, and Ametor and Ageleia, she that carries off the spoil.

And "Fortune, " for it decides mortal affairs.

And "Voice, " for there are seven tones of every voice, human and instrumental : because they are emitted by the seven planets, and form the music of the Spheres.

Also Tritogenia, because there are 3 parts of the Soul, the Intellectual, Irascible, and Epithymetic (desiring), and 4 most perfect virtues are produced. Just as of the three intervals, length, breadth, and depth, there are four boundaries in corporeal existence—point, line, superficies and solid.

It is called "Agelia " from Agelai, herds, as groups of stars were called by the Babylonian sages, over which herds ruled 7 angels.

Also Phylakikos=preserving "guardian, " because the Seven Planets direct and guide our universe.

Also Aegis, from Pallas Athene, or Minerva, the bearer of the breastplate or aegis, also Telesphoros, leading to the end, because the 7th month is prolific ; and Judgment, because their Physicians, looked for a crisis on the 7th day, in many diseases.

Among other curious problems and speculations the Pythagorean philosophers attempted to prove that offspring born at the full term, 9 months, or at 7 months, were viable, *i.e.*, might be reared, but not those born at 8 months, because 8 consists of two odd numbers (male only) 5 and 3; but in 9 and 7, male and female numbers are united, as 5+4=9 and 4+3 = 7, whilst eight can only be divided into two odd or two evens, *i.e.*, similar sexed numbers.

In respect to life and its divisions, they remarked the ages are measured by the number 7.

- In the first 7 years the teeth are erupted,
- second 7 years comes on ability to emit prolific seed,
- third 7 years, the growth of the beard as manhood,
- fourth 7 years strength reaches its maximum,
- fifth 7 years is the season for marriage,
- sixth 7 years the height of intelligence arrives,
- seventh 7 years, the maturity of reason,
- eighth 7 years, perfection of both,
- ninth 7 years, equity and mildness, passions become gentle,
- tenth 7 years, the end of desirable life.

Solon the Athenian Lawgiver, and Hippocrates the physician, also used this 7 year division of life.

The **Pleiades**, a group of seven stars in the constellation Taurus, was thought of mighty power over earthly destiny ; there were seven also of the Hyades, daughters of Atlas ; and the seven stars which guided the sailors. Ursa Major, in which the Hindoos locate the Saptarishi, seven sages of primitive wisdom, are a group of the first importance and are easily recognised.

Duncan, in his Astro Theology, gives 7 stages of life with associated planets; thus, Infancy, Moon, Lucina ; Childhood, Mercury, Knowledge; Youth, Venus, Love; Manhood, Sol; Full Strength, Mars ; Maturity of Judgment, Jupiter ; and Old Age, Saturn.

Some philosophers have said that our souls have 7 foci in the material body, *viz.,* the five senses, the voice, and the generative power.

The body has seven obvious parts, the head, chest, abdomen, two legs and two arms.

There are seven internal organs, stomach, liver, heart, lungs, spleen and two kidneys.

The ruling part, the head, has seven parts for external use, two eyes, two ears, two nostrils and a mouth.

There are seven things seen, body, interval, magnitude, colour, motion and permanency.

There arc seven inflections of the voice, the acute, grave, circumflex, rough, smooth, the long and the short sounds.

The hand makes seven motions ; up and down, to the right and left, before and behind and circular.

There are seven evacuations, tears from the eyes, mucus of the nostrils, the saliva, the semen, two excretions and the perspiration.

Modern medical knowledge corroborates the ancient dictum that in the seventh month the human offspring becomes viable.

Menstruation tends to occur in series of four times seven days, and is certainly related to Luna in an occult manner.

The lyre has 7 strings, corresponding to the Pleiades.

There are 7 vowels in English and some other tongues.

Theo, of Smyrna also notices that an average length of an adult's intestine is 28 feet, four times seven, and 28 also is a perfect number.

The number 7 is also associated with Voice and Sound, with Clio the Muse; with Osiris the Egyptian deity; with Nemesis, Fate,—Adrastia, not to be escaped from ; and with Mars.

As to the sacredness òf the number 7, note among the Hebrews oaths were confirmed by seven witnesses; or by seven victims offered in sacrifice; as see the covenant between Abraham and Abimelech with seven lambs, Genesis, cap. 21, v. 28, 21—28; the Hebrew word seven, also SH B O H, is derived from, or is a similar to SH B O to swear.

Clean beasts were admitted into the ark by sevens, whilst the unclean only in pairs.

The Goths had 7 Deities from whom come our names of week days ; Sun, Moon, Tuisco, Woden, Thor, Friga, Seatur, corresponding, of course to the planets.

Apollo, the Sun God, had a Greek title Ebdomaios, sevenfold. The Persian Mithras, a Sun God, had the number 7 sacred to him. Note the Mysterious Kadosch

Ladder of 7 steps ascent and 7 steps descent, the one side Oheb Eloah, Love of God ; the other Oheb Kerobo, love of the neighbour.

Plato, in his Timasus, teaches that from the number seven was generated the soul of the World, Anima Mundana (Adam Kadmon). The seven wise men of Greece were:

- Bias who said, " Most men are bad, " B.C. 5 50.
- Chilo, " Consider the end, " B.C. 590.
- Cleobulos, "Avoid extremes, " B.C. 580.
- Periander " Nothing is impossible to perseverance, " B.C. 600.
- Pittacus, " Know thy opportunity, " B.C. 569.
- Solon " Know thyself, " B.C. 600.
- Thales, " Suretyship is ruin, " B.C. 550.

The Seven Wonders of the World are thus enumerated :

1. Pyramids of Egypt.

2. Babylon, Gardens for Amytis.

3. Tomb of Mausolus, Kingl.of Caria, built by Artemisia, his Queen.

4. Temple of Diana at Ephesus, 552 B.C. Ctesiphon was the chief architect.

5. Colossus of Rhodes, an image of the sun god, Apollo, of brass, 290 B.C.

6. Statue of Zeus, by Phidias.

7. Pharos of Egypt, built by Ptolemy Philadelphus, of white marble, 283 B.C. or the Palace of Cyrus is sometimes substituted.

Sanskrit lore has very frequent reference to this number.

Sapta Rishi, seven sages

Sapta Kula, 7 castes

Sapta Loka, seven worlds

Sapta Para, 7 cities

Sapta Dwipa, seven holy islands

Sapta Arania, 7 deserts

Sapta Parna, 7 human principles.

Sapta Samudra, seven holy seas.

Sapta Vruksha, 7 holy trees

The Assyrian Tablets also teem with groups of sevens— 7 gods of sky ; 7 gods of earth ; 7 gods of fiery spheres. 7 gods maleficent; seven phantoms: spirits of seven heavens, spirits of seven earths.

Many Theosophists seem to assume that life on Earth came from the Pleiades. I see that in Dr. Thorlock's definition:

"He defines a mystic ' as a man, who, conscious of his affinity with all that exists from the Pleiades to the grain of dust, merged in the divine stream of life that pours through the universe, but perceiving also that the

purest spring of God bursts forth in his own heart,
moves onward across the world which is turned
towards what is limited and finite, turning his eye in
the centre of his own soul to the mysterious abyss,
where the infinite flows into the finite, satisfied in
nameless intuition of the sanctuary opened within
himself, and lighted up and embraced by a blissful love
of the secret source of his own being. "

- from *Theosophy or Psychological religion: the
Gifford lectures delivered before the University of
Glasgow in 1892*

In *The Theosophical Review,* Volume 32, page 20, we
see, "The air which we breathe and which sustains our
life is uniform and continuous with that which encircles
the **Pleiades.** "

...

I find some equally interesting concepts in *A
Theosophist's Point of View,* by James Albert Clark.

There, he says:

"Some carping criticism occasionally appears
concerning the enormous periods of time covered by
Hindu chronology, and Egyptian as well. It is not
absolutely essential that reliance be placed upon any
calculation, ancient or modern, for whether computed
in millions or billions of years the essentials of
Theosophy—the aiming toward the Perfect Man by
Reincarnation through the Law of Karma—would
remain unimpaired.

"Nevertheless, a curiosity is manifested by the "man on
the street " who asks concerning the theories which
have been put forward in certain Theosophical books,
the leading one being the quotation from the "Ocean of

Theosophy" by W. Q. Judge, and many wish he had not incorporated it in such dogmatic form:

'The real age of the world is asserted by Theosophy to be almost incalculable, and that of man as he is now formed is over eighteen millions of years.'

"The reasoning back of the above statement is not, or should not be a shock to our modern scientific thinking, though the genuine Yankee asks 'Why didn't you make it round numbers and call it 20,000,000 years and be done with it?'

"Simply because there was no valid reason to leave the problem as guess work. It was derived from a faithful traverse of the calculations of Maedler who proved to the satisfaction of many, if not all, that <u>our whole galaxy of stars is revolving in a mighty circle, the star Alcyone, of the **Pleiades**, being nearest the central point, and that eighteen million two hundred thousand years elapsed for one revolution around this distant center.</u>

"The credit of the mathematical problem may belong to Maedler, and others as well, who were working to the same end as is always the case as proved by Psychology.

"The real merit of the conclusion claimed for the deep brooding meditative Hindu mind was the concomitant study of Vibration.

"They reasoned with their time-honored acumen that the rate of vibration which ever determines Form, had not appreciably changed for this planet, during this one turn.

"Therefore, if the ratio of vibration kept uniform, so did man's erect form. This conclusion also is held tentatively, awaiting disproval.

"To follow out this reasoning let the reader ponder carefully the argument of Sir William Crookes, the great scientist, in his address to the Psychical Research Society wherein he demonstrates that if the rate of vibration on this globe was lowered but a degree, our forms would tend to the heaviness which would demand a support on all-fours; but let it, the rate, be raised but to an appreciable degree and we should become as the Greeks dreamed—'supremely tall and divinely fair,' and we could walk on eggs without crushing them. "

[*D.F.A. note:* That "tall and fair " reference suggests the Pleiadians, and also fits the description of Nordic Aliens (if they are, in fact, different from the Pleiadians) and perhaps other extraterrestrials.]

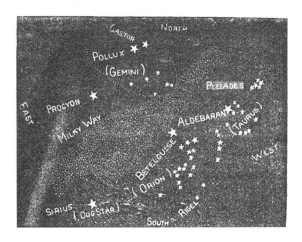

Scientific speculation continued in *The Esoteric,* Volume 4:

"The cluster of stars known as the Hyades, of which Aldebaran is the principal member, as well as the Pleiades, belong to the constellation of Taurus.

"Gemini is always quickly recognized by the two bright stars, Castor and Pollux ; the latter will be seen to possess much greater splendor than the former.

"The **Pleiades** cluster is the centre around which the visible universe revolves. As our sun, by his superior weight and volume, is sufficiently powerful to swing the Solar System in the multifarious movements exemplified by the several members, so the great power, the location of which is marked by the Pleiades, wields its force in the government of a Universe.

"Alcyone, the central sun, and principal star of this remarkable group, is estimated to possess a power and brilliancy equal to 12,000 of our sun! "

Returning to the Atlantis-Pleiades connection, I find this in the *Proceedings and transcripts*

"From China to ancient Britain prevailed the uniform belief that the ancestors of the human race came from Islands ; and from the time of Plato to the present, scores of volumes have been written on the subject.

"A celebrated French philosopher asks us, " Ne trouvez vous pas, Monsieur, quelque chose de singulier, dans cet amour ilea aneiens pour les isles ? Tout ce qu'il y a de sacre, de grand, et d'antique, s'y est passe : pourquoi les habitans du continent ont ils donne cet avantage aux isles, sur le continent meme '? "

"...Let us imagine that a migration did take place from Southern latitudes, and what would be the result ? The wanderers would bear with them a recollection of the Islands of the south, which they had left. They would see with dread, and remember long, that the stars that once rose on their right hand, had apparently reversed their movements. They might bring with them a year of seasons only suited to their former homes.

"The stars that once announced spring would long continue to be reverenced as the *Vergiliae*, though rising at the beginning of summer.

"Once marking the commencement of the year by appearing to their worshippers on the southern Halloween, and hence causing " the evening and the morning " to be "the first day, " the **Pleiades** would long retain their name as the Hesperides (the stars of the evening), even when they had ceased to regulate the year, when their "pleasant influences " had been forgotten ; when their rising in the evening was no longer reverenced, and their heliacal rising and setting in the morning was alone regarded ; when even that mode of regulating the seasons, had become disused, and the past influence and history of the Pleiads only existed as a matter of fable, and of doubt even to Astronomers themselves.

"Yet we find among ancient nations, that the Hesperides were connected most singularly with the traditions as to the primitive abodes of our race. The Southern Garden of the Hesperides recalls them to our mind ; while the name of these daughters of Atlas and of the Ocean, is blended with the memory of the lost Island of Atlantis. The key to many a mysterious myth will yet be found in the history of the seasons of the Pleiades.

"It is not less interesting to mark the wreck of the southern year, and of its New Year's festival of first fruits and of the dead, over which the Virgiliae once presided.

"In some cases, as in ancient Egypt, in Britain and Persia, we find it stranded in November as an ancient popular observance, though the year had long ceased to commence in that month.

"In other countries it drifted off from the autumn to form a New Year's festival in February.

"In one instance it shared the fate of the **Pleiades**, and took place, as the Lemuria of the Romans, in May, in which month it must have once been regulated by the heliacal rising of the *Hesperides* in the *morning* ; while the year of two seasons only survived in fables as to the two-faced Janus, or as matters of doubt and mystery to astronomers.

"So entirely have the history and 'the pleasant influences of the Pleiades' been forgotten, that the latest work on the astronomy of the ancients does not even refer to the primitive year commencing in November, or to the **Pleiades** as dividing its seasons.

"Even where history has preserved the tale of the Aztecs regulating their cycle in November by the culmination of the **Pleiades**, Greswell considers the circumstance so remarkable, as to deserve the special attention of Astronomers, and assumes that, if explained, it will favor his view as to there having been once a miraculous suspension of the laws that govern the universe.

"As the fables of Io and Icarus, hitherto unexplained, seem to relate to traditions as to a migration of races, and to changes in the seasons, it may be worth while to refer to them here.

"Io, the daughter of Inachus, is the same as Isis, who, we have seen, is plainly a mythical embodiment of the primitive year, and of its funereal agricultural New Year's festival.

"The name of the Hindoo Isis, *Cali,* means time. Mythology tells us that lo, <u>accompanied by the</u> **Pleiades**, after wandering over the whole earth, and being persecuted by Juno, on account of Jupiter, arrived at last at the Nile, where she was worshipped as Isis.

"To what can this refer, except to a year regulated by the **Pleiades**, having been brought from some distant country, and embodied in the myth of lsis. The fable of Io appears plainly in the Hindoo god, Carticeya, (the Pleiades?).

"A reference to the representation of him, given by Sir Wm. Jones, will leave but little doubt on this point. By his name, as well as by his crown of seven stars, he represents the **Pleiades**. By his faces looking in opposite directions, and by his six arms on each side, Janus bifrons, and the year of two seasons of six months each ; while in the peacock, on which he rides, we have the well known classical emblem of the many eyed Argus, the watchful keeper of Io. "

In a further curious note, the author says, "Now it is a curious coincidence, if nothing more, tbat in Africa, to this day, *Oro* is still worshipped, as he IS in Polynesia. *Isi* means a new period of time, *isi*mi a feast or festival, and *ikore* the harvest. "

I encourage you to read the entire article by Haliburton on the Festival of the Dead. It's in the appendix at the back of this book.

## The Pleiades and the Jehovah's Witnesses

'Judge' Joseph Franklin Rutherford was President of Watch Tower Bible and Tract Society from January 6, 1917 until his death on January 8, 1942.

During part of his presidency, he taught that Pleiades is the home of Jehovah God:

"The constellation of the seven stars forming the **Pleiades** appears to be the crowning center around which the known systems of the planets revolve.... It has been suggested, and with much weight, that one of the stars of that group is the dwelling place of Jehovah and the place of the highest heavens;...."

"The constellation of the **Pleiades** is a small one compared with others which scientific instruments disclose to the wondering eyes of man. But the greatness in size of other stars or planets is small when compared to the **Pleiades** in importance, because the **Pleiades** is the place of the eternal throne of God. "

*Reconciliation*, by J. F. Rutherford (1869 - 1942) 1928, p. 14.

However, by the mid-1950s, the importance of Pleiades was discounted by church publications.

From *The Watchtower*, 15 November 1953, page 703

Questions from Readers

"What is meant by 'binding the sweet influences of the Pleiades' or 'loosing the bands of Orion' or 'bringing forth Mazzaroth in his seasons' or 'guiding Arcturus with his sons,' as mentioned at Job 38:31, 32?-W. S., New York. "

In the reply, the author said that those views are not always astronomically sound and they're completely without Scriptural foundation.

He then said:

"Why? Because we do not know which stars or groups of stars are being referred to in these verses.

"The names Pleiades, Orion and Arcturus are not the names given in the Bible. Some translations make Mazzaroth refer to the signs of the Zodiac. "

As you've seen from my earlier quotations from the Vulgate, the Bible *does* list names.  The author continued:

"English translators have merely adopted these pagan names given to constellations or star groups and have inserted them in their translations in the place of the original names that appear in the Hebrew Scriptures, namely, Kimah, Kesil, Mazzaroth and 'Ayish.

"To just what stars or star groups these names refer we do not know today. "

The key *doctrinal* shift occurred in another paragraph in this supposed reply to a reader:

"Incidentally, **Pleiades** can no longer be considered the centre of the universe and it would be unwise for us to try to fix God's throne as being at a particular spot in the universe. "

Then, the author specifically mentionedDeut. 4:19; 2
Chron. 2:6; 6:18. I've copied those passages from the
King James Bible.

And lest thou lift up thine eyes unto heaven, and when
thou seest the sun, and the moon, <u>and the stars, even
all the host of heaven</u>, shouldest be driven to worship
them, and serve them, which the LORD thy God hath
divided unto all nations under the whole heaven. (Deut.
4:19)

But who is able to build him an house, <u>seeing the
heaven and heaven of heavens cannot contain him</u>?
who am I then, that I should build him an house, save
only to burn sacrifice before him? (2 Chron 2:6)

That's echoed in 2 Chron 6:18, But will God in very
deed dwell with men on the earth? behold, heaven and
the heaven of heavens cannot contain thee; how much
less this house which I have built!

From my viewpoint, that only says that God (or
perhaps Deity in general) is too large to be *limited* to
the heavens. <u>It doesn't address the issue of a star or
cluster being his home or point of origin.</u>

The heavens, at least as understood at the time the
Bible was written and compiled, usually references a
three-dimensional reality. Basing our understanding
on a literal interpretation of the Bible *can* conflict with
what we've learned about the Pleiades and the
Pleiadians.

## The Pleiades and the LDS (Mormon) Church

The following passages from the LDS (Mormon) Scriptures, The Pearl of Great Price, bear a strong resemblance to the information we have about Pleiades.

Was Abraham actually talking about Pleiades? Was there an error in translation?

1 And I, Abraham, had the Urim and Thummim, which the Lord my God had given unto me, in Ur of the Chaldees;

 2 And I saw the stars, that they were very great, and that <u>one of them was nearest unto the throne of God; and there were many great ones which were near unto it;</u>

3 And the Lord said unto me: These are the governing ones; and the name of the great one is <u>Kolob</u>, because it is near unto me, for I am the Lord thy God: <u>I have set this one to govern all those which belong to the same order as that upon which thou standest.</u>

 4 And the Lord said unto me, by the Urim and Thummim, that Kolob was after the manner of the Lord, according to its times and seasons in the revolutions thereof; that one revolution was a day unto the Lord, after his manner of reckoning, it being one thousand years according to the time appointed unto that whereon thou standest. This is the reckoning of the Lord's time, according to the reckoning of Kolob.

                    . . .

9 And thus there shall be the reckoning of the time of one planet above another, until thou come nigh unto Kolob, which Kolob is after the reckoning of the Lord's

time; which Kolob is set nigh unto the throne of God, to govern all those planets which belong to the same border as that upon which thou standest.

...

16 If two things exist, and there be one above the other, there shall be greater things above them; therefore Kolob is the greatest of all the Kokaubeam that thou hast seen, because it is nearest unto me.

Abr. 3: 1-4, 9, 16

13 But of the tree of knowledge of good and evil, thou shalt not eat of it; for in the time that thou eatest thereof, thou shalt surely die. Now I, Abraham, saw that it was after the Lord's time, which was after the time of Kolob; for as yet the Gods had not appointed unto Adam his reckoning.

Abr. 5: 13

When considering the word 'Kobol,' we need to look at similar sounding words, or how this might be a translation error.

In many cases, it appears that Joseph Smith may have been translating telepathically. For example, when he talked about the animals the early Americans used to transport, he describes them as horses. In that era, horses probably weren't in North America. However, if he was working with *visual* images and telepathy and saw someone native riding a large deer (one likely scenario), Smith may have assumed it was a horse.

The word 'Kolob' is remarkably (albeit dyslexically) like a term that appears in the Book of Enoch, often related to angel studies: Kokabel, alternately spelled Kaobiel, Kokabiel, Kawkabel, or Kakabel.

According to some Enochian scholars, that name represents the angel -- one of the 20 leaders named among the 200 Watchers -- responsible for teaching about the constellations.

If we use the Kaobiel spelling and pronunciation, there seems to be a connection to the word Kolob.

The question is: Are these semantic differences? Were Enoch, Smith and others using words that *all* relate to what we now know as the Pleiades and perhaps the Pleiadians?

Members of the LDS church don't seem to shy away from tackling this question. Within their scientific communities, even the most difficult aspects of Kolob have been discussed. The subject of Pleiades has definitely been on the table.

In *Astronomy, Papyrus, and Covenant,* Chapter 2 , Astronomy and the Creation in the Book of Abraham, contributing authors Michael D. Rhodes and J. Ward Moody say:

"Based on the assumption that 'governing' means gravitational attraction, there have been various guesses as to the location of Kolob. These have ranged from the star Alcyone in the **Pleiades** to the center of our own galaxy. However, recent observations have shown that rather than a star, there is a supermassive black hole at the center of our galaxy... " (emphasis added)

From 'Astronomy, Papyrus, and Covenant' by John Gee, and Brian M. Hauglid, copyright 2006, Brigham Young University, ISBN 0934893764.

For more, similar studies about Kolob -- including references that seem to suggest a connection with the Pleiades -- this book is worth reading.

Related notes:

In the (LDS) Book of Abraham, the word Kokaubeam is noted as the plural for stars.

It's also noteworthy that, according to LDS historian Hugh Nibley, Smith was quoting from the Book of Enoch during an era when most of that book had been lost.

Pleiadians experts and channelers, including Lyssa Royal and Keith Priest, have linked the Founders (from Lyra) and *the Watchers* described in Enoch.

### Recent Pleiades Activity

*Planets forming in Pleiades star cluster,*
*astronomers report*

By Stuart Wolpert / November 14, 2007

Rocky terrestrial planets, perhaps like Earth, Mars or Venus, appear to be forming or to have recently formed around a star in the Pleiades ('seven sisters') star cluster, the result of 'monster collisions' of planets or planetary embryos.

Astronomers using the Gemini Observatory in Hawaii and the Spitzer Space Telescope report their findings in an upcoming issue of the Astrophysical Journal, the premier journal in astronomy.

'This is the first clear evidence for planet formation in the Pleiades, and the results we are presenting may well be the first observational evidence that terrestrial planets like those in our solar system are quite common,' said Joseph Rhee, a UCLA postdoctoral scholar in astronomy and lead author of the research.

The Pleiades star cluster, in the constellation Taurus, is well-known in many cultures. It is named for the seven daughters of Atlas and Pleione, who were placed by Zeus among the stars in Greek mythology and is cited in the Bible — 'Can you bind the beautiful Pleiades? Can you loose the cords of Orion?' (Job 38:31). The automaker Subaru's name is the Japanese word for the Pleiades, Rhee said.

The Pleiades is probably the best known star cluster and the most striking to the naked eye. 'You've seen it many times, and it's now easily visible in the evening sky,' said research co-author Benjamin Zuckerman, UCLA professor of physics and astronomy.

Although referred to as the 'seven sisters,' 'the cluster actually contains some 1,400 stars,' said co-author Inseok Song, a staff scientist at NASA's Spitzer Science Center at the California Institute of Technology and a former astronomer with the Gemini Observatory.

Located about 400 light-years away, the Pleiades is one of the closest star clusters to Earth. One of the cluster's stars, known as HD 23514, which has a mass and luminosity a bit greater than those of the sun, is surrounded by an extraordinary number of hot dust particles — 'hundreds of thousands of times as much dust as around our sun,' Zuckerman said. 'The dust must be the debris from a monster collision, a cosmic catastrophe.'

The astronomers analyzed emissions from countless microscopic dust particles and concluded that the most likely explanation is that the particles are debris from the violent collision of planets or planetary embryos.

Song calls the dust particles the 'building blocks of planets,' which can accumulate into comets and small asteroid-size bodies and then clump together to form planetary embryos, eventually becoming full-fledged planets.

'In the process of creating rocky, terrestrial planets, some objects collide and grow into planets, while others shatter into dust,' Song said. 'We are seeing that dust.'

HD 23514 is the second star around which Song and Zuckerman recently have found evidence of terrestrial planet formation. They and their colleagues reported in the journal Nature in July 2005 that a sun-like star known as BD +20 307, located 300 light-years from Earth in the constellation Aries, is surrounded by one million times more dust than is orbiting our sun.

In an effort to uncover comparably dusty stars after their 2005 research, Rhee, Song and Zuckerman began looking through thousands of publicly accessible, deep-infrared images obtained by the Spitzer Space Telescope and soon discovered HD 23514. The astronomers then used the Gemini North telescope, located on Hawaii's dormant volcano Mauna Kea, to measure the heat radiation coming from the dust; the heat emerges at infrared wavelengths, just as the heat from our bodies does, Song said.

'The Gemini and Spitzer data were crucial in identifying and establishing the amount and location of dust around the star,' Song said.

While our sun is 4.5 billion years old, the Pleiades Aries stars are 'adolescents,' about 100 million and 400 million years old, respectively, Rhee said. Based on the age of the two stars and the dynamics of the orbiting dust particles, the astronomers deduce that most adolescent sun-like stars are likely to be building terrestrial-like planets through recurring violent collisions of massive objects. The cosmic debris from only a small percentage of such collisions can be seen at any one time — currently, only HD 23514 and BD +20 307 have visible debris.

'Our observations indicate that terrestrial planets similar to those in our solar system are probably quite common,' Zuckerman said.

The astronomers calculate that terrestrial planets or planetary embryos in the Pleiades collided within the last few hundred thousand years — or perhaps much more recently — but they cannot rule out the possibility that multiple, somewhat smaller collisions occurred.

Many astronomers believe our moon was formed through the collision of two planetary embryos — the young Earth and a body about the size of Mars. That

crash created tremendous debris, some of which
condensed to form the moon and some of which went
into orbit around the young sun, Zuckerman said.

By contrast, the collision of an asteroid with Earth 65
million years ago, the most favored explanation for the
final demise of the dinosaurs, was a mere pipsqueak, he
said.

'Collisions between comets or asteroids wouldn't
produce anywhere near the amount of dust we are
seeing,' Song said.

HD 23514 and BD +20 307 are by far the dustiest not-
so-young stars in the sky. 'Nothing else is even close,'
Song said.

Very young stars — those 10 million years old or
younger — may have a similar amount of dust around
them as a result of the star-formation process.
However, by the time a star is 100 million years old,
this 'primordial' dust has dissipated because the dust
particles get blown away or dragged onto the star, or
the particles clump together to form much larger
objects.

'Unusually massive amounts of dust, as seen at the
Pleiades and Aries stars, cannot be primordial but
rather must be the second-generation debris generated
by collisions of large objects,' Song said.

The Pleiades have been considered important by many
cultures throughout history.

'To the Vikings, the Pleiades was Freyja's hens,' Rhee
said. In Bronze Age Europe, the Celts and others
associated the Pleiades with mourning and funerals
because the cluster rose in the eastern night sky
between the autumnal equinox and the winter solstice,
which was a festival devoted to the remembrance of the

dead. The ancient Aztecs of Mexico and Central America based their calendar on the Pleiades.

The astronomers' research results are based on mid- and far- infrared observations made with the Gemini 8-meter Frederick C. Gillett Telescope at Gemini North and the space-based infrared observatories Infrared Astronomical Satellite (IRAS), Infrared Space Observatory (ISO) and NASA's Spitzer Space Telescope.

**The Gemini Observatory** is an international collaboration utilizing two identical 8-meter telescopes. The Frederick C. Gillett Gemini Telescope is located at Mauna Kea, Hawaii (Gemini North); the other is at Cerro Pachón in central Chile (Gemini South). Together they provide full coverage of both hemispheres of the sky. Both telescopes incorporate new technologies that allow large, relatively thin mirrors under active control to collect and focus both optical and infrared radiation from space.

**UCLA** is California's largest university, with an enrollment of nearly 37,000 undergraduate and graduate students. The UCLA College of Letters and Science and the university's 11 professional schools feature renowned faculty and offer more than 300 degree programs and majors. UCLA is a national and international leader in the breadth and quality of its academic, research, health care, cultural, continuing education and athletic programs. Four alumni and five faculty have been awarded the Nobel Prize.

## Photo and graphics credits

Portrait of Dr. Francis Crick, courtesy of the Public Library of Science, Siegel RM, Callaway EM: *Francis Crick's Legacy for Neuroscience: Between the α and the Ω.* PLoS Biol 2/12/2004: e419. http://dx.doi.org/10.1371/journal.pbio.0020419; photo by Marc Lieberman.

Tau-shaped crozier: Crozier of Saint w:Dimitrii Rostovskii the Miracle Worker. Museum inventory number 788. In the Rostov museum. Rostov Velikiy. Photograph by Sergei Mikhailovich Prokudin-Gorskii, 1911.

Crosiere of arcbishop Heinrich of Finstingen 1260-1286, from Limoges, middle of the 13th century. Located in the Domschatz Trier. Courtesy of Wikipedia user: Chris 73.

Modern photographs of Pleiades courtesy of NASA.

CroCro font courtesy of CroCroTraUmAx Project, http://www.mmparis.com/crocrotraumax/

**APPENDIX ONE** begins on the next printed page and is a paper by R. G. Haliburton on the Festival of the Dead.

## Haliburton *on the Festival of the Dead.*

Art. VII.—*The Festival of the Dead.** By R. G. Haliburton, F.S.A.

In European Calendars, the last day of October, and the first and second days of November, are designated as the Festivals of All Halloween, All Saints, and All Souls.

Though they have hitherto never attracted any special attention, and have not been supposed to have been connected with each other, they originally constituted but one commemoration of three days duration, known among almost all nations as "the festival of the dead," or the "feast of ancestors."

It is now, or was formerly, observed at or near the beginning of November by the Peruvians, the Hindoos, the Sandwich Islanders, the people of the Tonga Islands, the Australians, the ancient Persians, the ancient Egyptians, and the northern nations of Europe, and continued for three days among the Japanese, the Hindoos, the Australians, the ancient Romans, and the ancient Egyptians.

Halloween is known among the Highlanders by a name meaning the consolation of the spirits of the dead, and is with them, as with the Cinghalese,† the Sandwich Islanders, and almost every race among whom the festival

---

* At the suggestion of the writer, the above paper was substituted for one read before the Institute, which had been privately printed. In the previous one, on "New materials for the History of man, derived from a comparison of the customs and superstitions of nations," it was endeavored to show that the source of these superstitions, so far from being "absolutely unattainable," as it has been hitherto considered by all who have treated of them, could be arrived at by a comparison of the customs of civilized and savage races; and that those superstitions, being possessed of a marvellous vitality, are valuable historical memorials of primitive society.

As an illustration of the duration and universality of primitive superstitions and customs, those connected with the habit of saying "God bless you!" to a person who sneezes, were selected. This absurd custom, referred to by Homer, and found in Europe, Asia, Africa, Polynesia and America, was traced to a belief found in the Arctic regions, Australia, and Central Africa, (and it might have been added in Ireland), that death and disease are not the result of natural but of supernatural causes; and that when a person sneezes, he is liable to be a victim of the spirits, or as the Celtic race express it, "to be carried off by the fairies." It was also argued that this custom, the trivial nature of which precludes the idea that it could have been borrowed by nations from each other, or that nature can everywhere have suggested it to the human race, plainly must have been inherited from a common source, and is a very conclusive argument in favor of the unity of origin of our race. These views have been confirmed by the observations of Captains Speke and Grant—(see Illustrated London News, July 4, 1863, p 23.) An interesting little work by W. R. Wylde, on "Irish Popular Superstitions," published by William S. Orr & Co., London—which the writer was unable to procure until after the paper was read before the Nova Scotian Institute—supplies very curious facts, which corroborate his conclusions as to the origin of this custom. See from p. 120 to 125; also p. 51 to 58. See also Strada's Prolusiones—*Our sternuentes salutentur* lib. iii. Præl. iv.

† See Brady's Clavis Calendaria, as to Oct. 31st.

## Haliburton *on the Festival of the Dead.*

is observed, connected with a harvest home, or, south of the equator, with a first fruits celebration.    An old writer asks why do we suppose that the spirits of the dead are more abroad on Halloween than at any other time of the year?[*]  and so convinced are the Finns and the Irish peasantry of the fact, that they discreetly prefer remaining at home on that ill-omened night.

The Halloween torches of the Irish, the Halloween bonfires of the Scotch, the Coel Coeth fires of the Welsh, and the Tindle fires of Cornwall, lighted at Halloween, are clearly memorials of a custom found almost everywhere at the celebration of the festival of the dead.    The origin of the lanthorn festival has never yet been conjectured.    It will be found, I believe, to have originated in the wide-spread custom of lighting bonfires at this festival.

The Church of de Sens, in France, was endowed by its founder in the days of Charlemagne, for the purpose of having mass said for the dead, and the grave yard visited on All Halloween.[†]  Wherever the Roman-Catholic Church exists, solemn mass for *all souls* is said on the first day of November; on that day the gay Parisians, exchanging the boulevard for the cemetary, lunch at the graves of their relatives, and hold unconsciously a funeral feast on the very same day that savages in far distant quarters of the globe observe in a similar manner their "feast of ancestors."[‡]

Even the Church of England, which rejects *All Souls*, as based on a belief in purgatory, and as being a creation of popery, devoutly clings to All Saints, which is clearly a relic of primeval heathenism.

On All Souls day, the English peasant goes *a-souling*, begging for " a soul cake for all Christen souls."    He has very little suspicion that he is preserving a heathen rite, the meaning of which is not to be found in the book of common prayer, but (as I shall hereafter show) is to be discovered in the sacred books of India, in which country the consecrated cake is still offered, as it has been for thousands of years in November, to the souls of deceased ancestors.    But, though the festival of the dead is so generally observed in November, there are some exceptions.    Thus it was observed in February by the Greeks, the Romans, the Persians, and the Algonquins, and in August by the Japanese and Chinese.    The traces of its being observed in May are very few, and those of its being

* See Brand's Popular Antiquities, v.I, p. 388, 396. (Ed. 1853.)

† Hodie in Ecclesia Senonensi, sit Anniversarium solemne, et generale pro de‐functis.—*Thiers' Traité des Superstitions*, iii. 98.

‡ Atlantic Monthly for May, 1862.

## Haliburton *on the Festival of the Dead.*

held at any other times of the year, are of exceedingly rare occurrence. Before, therefore, I can attempt to treat of the festival of the dead, or refer to its origin and history, and the influence it has exerted on ancient mythology, it is necessary to confine this paper simply to questions connected with the Calendar, and the times when the festival is found to be observed. It is important to trace the ancient November festival to the primeval year, which must have ,fixed it in that month among races South, as well as North of the Equator. This year, I believe I have succeeded in discovering; and, as it appears to have originated in, or at least only now exists in, the Southern hemisphere, I have designated it as the Primitive Southern year. It is also necessary to show that the festival of the dead, occurring in February or August, indicates a change having taken place, and a more recent year commencing in February having been substituted. As we only find this year north of the Equator (so far as I have been able to learn), I have designated it as the Primitive Northern year.

Wherever the festival occurs in November, it is, or at least originally was, the new year's festival, of the primitive Southern year. Where it is held in February, it is, or once was, the commemoration of the commencement of the Northern year.

As the mode of investigation pursued on this point materially adds to the credibility of my conclusions, I may be pardoned for referring to it.

The startling fact that " this feast was celebrated among the ancient Peruvians at the same period, and on the same day that Christians solemnize the commemoration of the dead, (2d November)"* at once drew my attention to the question, how was this uniformity in the time of observance preserved, not only in far distant quarters of the globe, but also through that vast lapse of time since the Peruvian, and the Indo-European first inherited this primeval festival from a common source?

It was plain that this singular uniformity could never have been preserved by means of the defective solar year in vogue among ancient nations. How then could this result have been produced? It was apparent that the festival must have been regulated by some visible sign, or mark, that nature had supplied—such as the rising of some constellation.

Remembering the ancient traditions as to the Pleiades, I naturally turned my attention to them. Professor How kindly offered to ascertain from an excellent astronomer whether the Pleiades could have ever risen in November in Asia or Europe. I was fortunately, however, able to save

---

* Peruvian Antiquities, by M. Rivero and Von Tschudi, translated by Dr Hawks, New York, 1855, p. 134.

## Haliburton *on the Festival of the Dead.*

that gentleman the calculation.    On turning to Bailly's *Astronomie Indienne*,* I found him state that the most ancient year, as regulated by the calendar of the Brahmins of Tirvalore, began in November, and I was much gratified at finding that, in that Calendar, the month of November is called Cartiguey, *i. e.* the month of the Pleiades,—a circumstance which M. Bailly says, would seem to indicate that that Constellation by their rising or setting in that month, must have regulated the commencement of the ancient year in November.

But here a fresh difficulty arose, as respects the Calendar.    To suppose that the Pleiades rose in that month, and commenced the year in the autumn, was not only opposed to ancient traditions respecting them, and to their name as the Stars of Spring ( *Vergiliæ* ), but also to their actual movements, at the present day at least.

We could not assume that great astronomical changes could ever have produced this result.  How then could we account for the anomaly ?  I discovered the clue in extending my researches to the Southern hemisphere, where I found the festival of the dead to occur in November, and to be the vernal New Year's festival of a year commencing in November, and regulated by the rising of the Pleiades *in the evening*.    Before concluding this prefatory paper, it may be as well to state that the whole subject referred to by me, both as regards the primitive New Year Festival of the Dead, and the primitive year, has altogether escaped the observation of the learned.    De Rougemont, in his " Peuple Primitif, " published at Paris in 1856, has, out of three volumes, not devoted as many pages to " Les Fêtes des Morts," though they are unquestionably the most remarkable memorials we possess of Le peuple Primitif.   Festivals connected with the seasons, he says, cannot now be investigated, from our ignorance of the primitive calendar ; and he therefore only selects those that took place at the time of the Vernal Equinox, and the Summer Solstice, *i. e.* associated with a solar year, and hence of a comparatively recent date, and subsequent to those of the two primitive calendars which I have referred to.

" Nous ne pouvons ici faire une étude spéciale de celles, qui se rapportent avant tout aux saisons ; les calendriers des anciens nous sont trop imparfaitment connus, pour que nous puissions espérer de reconstruire celui du peuple primitif."†

The primitive year of two seasons, commencing in November, and the connection of the Pleiades with the primeval calendar, are not even referred to in the latest work on the astronomy of the ancients, published last year

* Vol. 1. p. xxxi. 28, 134.
† Vol. 1. p. 523.

## Haliburton *on the Festival of the Dead.*

in Paris.* Though very many remarkable facts in the history of the
calendar, and of our race, to which the study of the festival of the dead
has afforded me a clue, are referred to by Greswell in his learned works
on the Calendars of the Ancients, he has attempted to explain them by
resorting to the miracles in the Bible—as to the sun having stood still or
gone back on certain occasions—events which he contends must not only
have disturbed, but have even left their impress on the calendars of the
ancients.    But they are, I believe, capable of a more common-place solution.    I trust that I shall be able to prove that these subjects are susceptible
of an explanation, without having, with Greswell, to refer to miracles
in the days of Hezekiah, or with Ovid, to leave the knotty point to be
unravelled by the Gods—

> " Dicta sit unde dies, quæ nominis extet origo
> Me fugit, ex aliquo est invenienda deo."†

### THE FESTIVAL OF THE DEAD BROUGHT TO EUROPE AND ASIA BY A MIGRATION OF RACES FROM THE SOUTHERN HEMISPHERE.

" Mudan de pays y de estrellas."‡—*Garcillasso de la Vega.*

" Who can restrain the pleasant influences of the Pleiades ?" we are
asked in the book of Job, the most ancient production of sacred or pro-
fane literature.    "The lights in the firmaments of the heavens," "for
signs and for seasons, and for days, and for years," are supposed to have
reference to that constellation, as well as to the sun and moon, for in early
ages neither the sun nor the moon could have indicated the length of the
year, or its division into seasons.    The extreme veneration of remote
antiquity for the Pleiades, or *Vergiliæ*, for having marked the seasons,
and the beginning of spring, are amongst the most venerable traditions of
our race, and are now only realized among Australian savages, who still
worship the Pleiades as announcing spring, "and as being very good to
the blacks ;" and at their culmination hold a great New Year's corroboree
in November, in honor of the *Mormodellick*, as they call that time-honored
constellation.    The name given to these stars by the Romans, *Vergiliæ*,
is plainly connected with the strange tradition of Northern natives, of the
Pleiades having marked the commencement of spring.    They are popu-

* " Antiquité des Races Humaines.   Reconstitution de la Chronologie, et de l'
Histoire des Peuples Primitifs.   Par l' examen des documents originaux, et par
l' Astronomie,"—by Rodier.
† Fasti, Lib. v.
‡ They change their country and their stars.

## Haliburton *on the Festival of the Dead.*

larly known, from France to India, by the same name—a circumstance which proves, says Mr. Bailly,[*] that our first knowledge of these stars was derived from the most ancient nations of Asia.

The question naturally suggests itself, whence arose this veneration for a constellation, that among us, at least, are no longer reverenced? When and where can they have marked the beginning of spring, and what were those "pleasant influences," referred to in the book of Job, and still celebrated by Australian savages?

So far from rising in Europe or Asia in the spring, they first appear in June, a summer month. How could the *Vergiliæ*, then, have acquired their name, as the stars of spring? It is plain that they could not have marked a vernal commencement of the year, as the most ancient year commenced in the autumn, and among most ancient nations we find traces of a traditionary or civil year commencing in the autumn.

We also find traces of a very singular year of six months, the very existence of which Sir Cornewall Lewis has somewhat hastily questioned. "These abnormal years," he tells us, "are designated by Censorinus as involved in the darkness of remote antiquity."[†] Dupuis suggests that we must turn to the Pleiades, as well as to other constellations, to account for these "abnormal years," as well as for the ancient year commencing in the autumn,—"pour expliquer les fictions relatives à ce commencement, d'année, soit chez les Juifs, soit chez les autres peuples, qui ont eu le commencement d'année en automne. Tels etaient ceux qui avaient des années de six mois."[‡] In confirmation of his conjecture, I have found that in the Arabian calendar of lunar mansions, which is made up of two divisions, one belonging to summer, and the other to winter,—one of the mansions is designated by the name of the Pleiades. Let us see if his suggestion will prove equally correct respecting the autumnal year; and let us endeavor to find in that constellation a clue to the remarkable circumstance of the festival of the dead having been observed in Hindostan, Peru, Ceylon, Egypt, and Europe, in November.

I may here state that the classical nations of antiquity, with whom the influence of the Pleiades was rather a matter of tradition than of practical use, when they spoke of the rising of the Pleiades, referred to the

---

[*] This name was the *Hen and Chickens;* among the Hindoos, Pillalou Codi; among the Jews, Succoth Benoth (?); among the Italians, Gallineta, and among the French, *La pousinière.* See Dupuis De l' origine de tous les Cultes, ix., 192. Bailley's Astronomie Indienne, I. xxxv., 134, 328. See, however, Landseer's Sabæan Researches, Lecture XI., p. 19.

[†] Historical Survey of the Astronomy of the Ancients, p. 31.

[‡] L'Origine de tous Les Cultes, v. 1, p. 104.

## Haliburton *on the Festival of the Dead.*

heliacal rising of the constellation in the morning, *i. e.* the time, when at dawn, the stars where first visible—*

·" The grey dawn and the Pleiades
Shedding sweet influence."

This took place in the middle of May, 2000 years ago, and marked the beginning of summer in the South of Europe and Asia.† But we must conclude either that the Pleiades must have once, in some other manner, than by their heliacal rising, indicated the beginning of spring, or else that there must have been, by a long lapse of years, a change in their movements, that rendered their rising inconsistent with their very name as the stars of spring. It must, however, have been nearly 5000 years since the heliacal rising of the Pleiades occurred at the beginning of April, and even then it could not have indicated the commencement of seed time in the South of Asia and of Europe, or marked the beginning of spring. Their name, the Hesperides, too, would seem to connect them with the evening rather than the morning. But, if at such a remote era, the Pleiades regulated the seasons by their heliacal rising at that time of the year, they must have left their impress on primitive calendars, and traces of the connection of the calendar with the heliacal rising of the Pleiades, would still be found among many races, either in their names for March or April, or at least in their traditions as to the time when their year once commenced. But this is not the case. There are no traces of a primitive year in general use in remote antiquity, commencing in March, April or May; the only apparent exception being the solar year, regulated by the vernal Equinox, which was of comparatively recent invention.

But on examining the calendars of ancient races, we find in Persia India, Egypt and Peru, that the month in which our first of November festival would fall, bears in its very name a singular impress of its former connection, either with the Pleiades or the festival of the dead.

In the most ancient calendar in India, the year commenced in the month of November, which bears the name of Cartiguey, *i. e.*, the Pleiades; a constellation which, Bailly suggests, must have by their rising or setting at that time, once have regulated the primitive year. We

---

* Pleiades adspecies omnes, totumque sororum
Agmen; ubi ante Idus nox erit una super.
Tunc mihi non dubiis autoribus incipit aetas,
Et tepidi finem tempora veris habent.

*Ov. Fast., Lib.* v.

† See as to the cosmical and heliacal risings of stars, Greswell's Fasti Catholici. v. III, p. 18.

## Haliburton *on the Festival of the Dead.*

find also that towards the end of October, the Hindoo like ourselves, have three days which are connected with the festival of the dead.

In the ancient Egyptian calendar the same resemblance can be traced between the name of the Pleiades, which among the Hebrews and Chaldeans is Athor-aye, with that of the Egyptian month of November, which is Athor.    The Arab name for the Pleiades, Atauria, also suggests a resemblance.

In November took place the primeval festival of the dead, clad in a veil of Egyptian mythology.    The Isia, the solemn mourning for the God Osiris, " the Lord of Tombs," lasted for three days, and began at sunset, like the Lemuria of the Romans, and the festival of the dead among the Persians and other nations.

The singular custom of counting the days from the sunset of the preceding day, or the noctidiurnal system, was so universal, that Greswell refers to it as a conclusive proof of the unity of origin of our race. *The bible tells us, "the evening and the morning were the first day." Our words "fortnight" and "sennight," are traces of this primitive custom ; and he might have added the first day of our festival of the dead, a still stronger illustration, as it is called Halloween.   The origin of this system has not been explained by Greswell.   He tells us, however, of the Egyptian belief, that whoever could discover the origin of the Isia, or the Egyptian festival of the dead, would know why the day came to be counted from the evening of the preceding day.   Hence the origin of this wide-spread noctidiurnal system is to be found (if the Egyptians were correct) in whatever caused the festival of the dead to commence at sunset, or with a Halloween.

Let us turn to the primitive races of the Southern Hemisphere to find a solution.—

1st—For the festival of the dead being connected with an agricultural celebration.   2d—For its being held in November.   3rd—For its commencing with a Halloween.   4th—For the primitive year commencing in November.   5th—For the Pleiades being connected with that month. 6th—For their being reverenced as the *Vergiliæ* and Hesperides, the stars of the spring and the evening.   7th—For the "abnormal year" of six months, found North of the Equator.

A reference to the Australians and Pacific Islanders, will enable us to give a very simple explanation for these various points, without imagining that miracles must have given rise to some, or that we must leave the solution of others to the gods.

* See Volmer's Wörterbuch der Mythologie, verb Athor, p. 371.

## Haliburton *on the Festival of the Dead.*

We find that, among these Southern races,* when the Pleiades are in the evening first visible at the horizon, which is at the beginning of November, they mark the beginning of the year, and the vernal new year's festival, a feast consecrated to first fruits, and to the dead. As long as at evening they continue visible, they mark a season called *the Pleiades above.* When they cease to be visible in the evening, the second season commences of *the Pleiades below* : these seasons nearly equally dividing the year. Hence we can understand why tradition has connected the Pleiades with November, as the first month of the year, has preserved their name as the stars of the evening and of the spring, and has caused the festival of the dead to commence in the evening, or with a Halloween. We can also understand how the year of six months arose, that has so puzzled Astronomers.

In the voluminous report on the Aborigines, by a Committee of the Legislative Council of Victoria, Session 1858-9, we find W. Hull, Esquire, J. P., a gentleman who has written a work on the Aborigines, stating "their grand corroborees are held only in the spring, when the Pleiades are generally most distinct ; and their corroboree is a worship of the Pleiades as a constellation, which *announces spring.* Their monthly corroboree is in honor of the moon." (p. 9.)

In another place Mr. Hull says, "referring again to their worship of the stars, I may mention that one night I showed Robert Cunningham the Pleiades, and he said ' they were the children of the moon, and very good to the black fellows,'—a remark that recals to our mind ' the pleasant influences of the Pleiades.'"

C. J. Tyers, Esq., Commissioner of Crown Lands, Alberton, (p. 79,) says in confirmation of the foregoing,—"Regarding their religious practices very little is known, so little that Europeans generally believe them to be devoid of any. Yet they do, according to their manner, worship the hosts of heaven, and believe particular constellations rule natural causes. For such they have names ; and *sing and dance to gain the favor of the Pleiades,* (Mormodellick,) the constellation worshipped by one body as the giver of rain." Now the Pleiades are most distinct at the beginning of the spring month of November, when they appear at the horizon in the evening, and are visible all night. Hence their vernal festival of the Pleiades takes place in honor of the Vergiliæ, the stars of spring, at the beginning of November, the very month called in the calen-

---

* I have only been able to fix the date of this festival among the natives of the Society and Tonga Islands. The difficulty of procuring necessary works of reference in a Colony will plead, I trust, an excuse for many omissions.

## Haliburton *on the Festival of the Dead.*

dar of the Brahmins of Tirvalore, the month of the Pleiades, and among
the ancient Egyptians connected with the name of that constellation.

But we are told by another gentleman examined by the committee,
that all the corroborees of the natives are connected with a worship of the
dead,* and *last three days.* If this be the case, is it not somewhat
startling to find that Australian savages, at or near the time of Halloween,
All Saints and All Souls, also consecrate three days to the memory of the
dead, as a vernal New Year's celebration, regulated by the time-honored
Pleiades,—and like the northern festival of the dead, beginning in the
evening, or with a Halloween?

> "Hinc ubi protulerit formosa ter Hesperus ora,
> Ter dederint Phœbo sidera victa locum ;
> Ritus erit veteris nocturna Lemuria sacri ;
> Inferias tacitis Manibus illa dabunt."†

In the Tonga Islands, which belong to the Feejee group, the festival of
Inachi, a vernal first fruits celebration, and also a commemoration of the
dead, takes places towards the end of October,‡ and commences at sunset.

"The Society Islanders," Ellis tells us, "divided the year into two
seasons of the Pleiades or Matarii. The first they called the *Matarii i
nia*, or the *Pleiades above.*" It commenced where, in the evening these
stars appeared, at or near the horizen," (*i. e.* at or near the beginning of
November), and the half year during which, immediately after sunset,
they were seen above the horizon, was called *Matarii i nia.* The other
seasons commenced when, at sunset these stars are invisible, and continued
until at that hour they appeared again above the horizon. This season
was called *Matarii i raro, i. e. "the Pleiades below."* The Pleiades
are visible at the horizon in the evenings at the beginning of November.
They then culminate near midnight, and are visible till morning. Ellis
says that this year began in May ; but it is evident that what he calls the
first season, "the Pleiades above," commenced at or near the beginning
of November, and the second division must have begun towards the end
of April, or early in May. If they appear at the horizon in the evening,
on 5th November, they continue visible at that time till the 24th April
following. But, not only was the month of November connected with the

---

* In confirmation of this, a member of the N. S. Institute, who has been at these
annual corroborees, tells me, that as the natives for these occasions paint a white
stripe over their arms, legs and ribs, they appear, as they dance by their fires at
night, like so many skeletons rejoicing. The custom, however, is peculiar, I believe, to Australia. *White* paint is used for mournful, and *red* for joyful festivals.
See Report on Aborigines, p. 70, 94.

† Ov. Fast., Lib. v.

‡ Mariner's Tonga Islands, p. 157, 381, 385.

## Haliburton *on the Festival of the Dead.*

rising of the Pleiades, but also with a festival of the dead, and a first fruits celebration, as among the people of the Tonga Islands.

"The most singular of their stated festivals was the ripening or completing of the year. Vast numbers of both sexes attended it; the women, however, were not allowed to enter the sacred enclosure. A sumptuous banquet was then held. This ceremony was viewed as a *national acknowledgment to the Gods*. When the prayers were finished, and the banquet ended, a usuage prevailed *resembling much the popish custom of mass for souls in purgatory*. Each one returned to his home or family marae, there to offer special prayers for the spirits of departed relatives." Ellis does not tell us to what mode of dividing the year he refers (for they appear to have had three); but, as the Inachi of the Tonga Islands, a precisely similar celebration, as well as the festival of the Pleiades in Australia, took place near the beginning of November, we may assume that this was the new year's festival of the seasons of the Pleiades.

Let us turn from the Islands of the Pacific to Peru, and there we find this primitive calendar of two seasons marked by a new year's festival of the dead, occurring in November; and celebrated at precisely the same time as in Europe and Polynesia.

The month in which it occurs, says Rivero, "is called Aya-marca, from Aya, a corpse, and *marca*, carrying in arms. because they celebrated the solemn festival of the dead, with tears, lugubrious songs, and plaintive music; and it was customary to visit the tombs of relations, and to leave in them food and drink. *It is worthy of remark that the feast was celebrated among the ancient Peruvians at the same period, and on the same day, that Christians solemnize the commemoration of the dead*, (2nd November)."

Finding the festival held at the beginning of November, I felt convinced that it never could have been fixed in that month by a solar year, such as was in use in Peru, but that it must have been originally the New Year's festival of the year or seasons of the Pleiades, that must have once been in use in that country. Subsequent investigations bore out the conclusion.

M. Rivero tells us that in November took place the termination of the year and of seed time. Garcilasso* bears distinct testimony to the existence of a traditionary year of seasons.

* Book II. ch. xi. Garcilasso says the harvest time was in March, but Rivero (p. 132) places it in May.

## Haliburton *on the Festival of the Dead.*

"Yet, for all this sottish stupidity, the Incas had observed that the Sun accomplished his course in the space of a year, which they called *huata ;* though the commonality *divided it only by its seasons,* and reckoned their year to end or be finished with their harvest," (*i. e.* in May.)

Here we have the year ending with the months of November, and May, a plain proof that the Southern years of the Pleiades ending in November and May, must have existed there before the Incas invented or introduced the solar year; and were the seasons referred to by Garcilasso. As the festival of the dead is, however, the new year's festival of the year of the Pleiades, we may assume that it must have, in Peru, originally marked the commencement of the year at the beginning of November. Wherever the festival of the dead occurs in November, even among nations now far north of the equator, the same inference may, I believe, be adduced. The race by whom it is preserved must have once regulated that festival in November, by the rising of the Pleiades, like the Australians and the Pacific Islanders.

In Persia we find a singular light thrown on the calendar by the festival of agriculture and of death celebrated south of the equator. In the ancient calendar November was consecrated to the angel who presided over agriculture and death. We have seen that the month in which this festival occurred in Peru, was called "the month of carrying corpses." The month of November, was formerly called in Persia Mordâd, the month of the angel of death. . In spite of the calendar having been changed, at the same time as in Peru, the festival of the dead took place as a new year's festival, (although the year no longer commenced then.) It is called by some writers the *Nouruz of the Magi,* because the Magi still adhered to their primitive new year's festival.[*] It commenced in the evening with a Halloween, which was regarded as peculiarly sacred. "Unde hujus diei *Vespera* quibusdam Persarum, peculiari nomine signatur Phristâph.[†] Bonfires were lighted at this festival as they are in Britain, and in most portions of the globe, at this season of the year.[‡]

In Ceylon, Sir Emerson Tennent says a festival is held that is a species of harvest home and a commemoration of the dead. It must, however, be rather a first fruits celebration, like that of nations south of the equator, as the harvest is over in May or June. This festival of agriculture and of death took place at the beginning of November.[§]

We now turn to Mexico, and there we find that the great festival of the

---

[*] Rel. Vet. Persarum, 238.  [†] Id. 237.  [‡] Id. 249.
[§] Tennent's Christianity in Ceylon, 202, 228. Forbes' Ceylon, 2, 322. See Mahavansi transl'd. by Upham, III. 164.

## Haliburton *on the Festival of the Dead.*

Mexican cycle was held at the beginning of November, and was regulated by the Pleiades. It began at sunset; and at midnight, as the constellation approached the zenith, a human victim, Prescott says, was offered up to avert the dread calamity which they believed impended over the human race. This belief* was so remarkable that I cannot omit a reference to it here. They had a tradition that at that time the world had been previously destroyed; and they dreaded lest a similar catastrophe would, at the end of a cycle, annihilate the human race.

Now it is most remarkable to find that the Egyptians, with their Isia, or new year's festival of agriculture, and of the dead, that took place on the 17th day of November, associated traditions as to the deluge, and it is still more surprising to find that the 17th day of November is the very day on which, the Bible tells us, the deluge took place.†

Greswell has devoted several chapters, and much learning, to the 17th day of November (Athor),‡ to show how remarkable a landmark it has always been, through a long lapse of centuries, for the corrections of the Egyptian calendar, and he derives from it some curious arguments in support of his view. De Rougemont and other writers have referred to this day, but have thrown no light upon it. They seem, however, not to have observed that even among the Persians the same day was peculiarly venerated. Hyde says that in the ancient Persian calendar the 17th day of November was held so sacred, that all favors asked by rulers were granted on that day;§ but why it was so venerated he does not attempt to conjecture. Even tradition has been unable to preserve the history of this day, that must be sought for in the very earliest ages of the world, or among

---

* Prescott's Conq. of Mexico, I., b. 1, ch. iv.

† While the above was going through the press, as I was convinced that the memory of the deluge had been thus preserved among the Hebrews, Egyptians, Greeks and Mexicans, in the traditions connected with the new year's festival, and that the date of the commencement of the deluge, the 17th day of the first month of the primitive year, was not of an historical but of an astronomical character, I more closely examined the Mosaical account of the deluge, and found my conjecture singularly verified. The deluge commenced on the 17th of the 2nd month of the Jewish year (*i. e.* November); the ark rested on Mount Ararat on the 17th day of the 7th month; and the dove returned with the olive branch on the 17th day of the 11th month. Though the connection of this with the traditions and calendars of heathen races is somewhat startling, I am convinced that should the study of *Ethology* afford a clue to the primeval origin of pagan idolatry, it will at the same time conclusively prove how entirely different and distinct must have been the source from which the Hebrews derived the great truths and principles of our religion.

‡ Those wishing to examine into these points, will find the following references bearing on them:—Greswell's Fasti Catholici, 1., 82, 152, 154, 168, 181, 196, 198, 200, 225, 228, 229, 343, 356 : II., 104, 115, 226; III., 88, 89, 112, 113, 131, 160, 166, 330, 405, 407, 413, 416 : IV. 173, 610. See Origines Kalendariæ Italicæ, I., 344, 348, 351 to 390, 423, 430 : III., 33, 460, 516.

§ See. Rel. Vet. Pers., p. 243.

## Haliburton *on the Festival of the Dead.*

the rudest existing types of man. In the mysteries of Isis, the goddess of agriculture and of death, the funereal part of the ceremonies, the lamentations and search for Orisis, commenced on the 17th and ended on the 19th. There was also an obsolete year of the Egyptians, which commenced, Greswell says, about the 18th of November.

Herodotus tells us, what is very plain, that Isis is the same as the Greek goddess Ceres, who, with her daughter Proserpine, presided over agriculture and the dead.*

Among the Greeks, besides existing in other ceremonies, the primeval new year's festival appears under a veil of mythology in all the ancient mysteries, but above all in the greatest of them, the Eleusinian. The Greeks, however, must have at some remote era changed the beginning of the year from the 17th of November to the 17th of February, when the Attic year commenced. On the 17th, 18th and 19th days of February, the funereal part of the Eleusinian mysteries, the lament for Proserpine, took place.

The Macedonians retained the primitive year beginning in November.† It is peculiarly interesting to note that with the new year's festival, the tradition as to the deluge was also transferred by the Athenians to the 17th day of February. Even in some other months, the 17th seems to to have been a conspicuous day in the Greek calendar. In Persia, in every month, there were three days of sadness and fasting; but as the 17th and 18th days were dies nefasti, on which no work was done, we may assume that the 19th was the ultima dies placandis manibus,‡ and the 17th, 18th and 19th were the days of mourning.§ In Europe, Asia and Africa, we find days in every month consecrated to the memory of the dead.

Let us now look south of the Equator for an explanation : 1st—Why the 17th, 18th and 19th of the month were so funereal. 2nd—Why the primitive year of the Egyptians and of other races, and their funereal mysteries, began on the 17th day of the month. 3rd—Why, not only at every new year's festival, but even monthly, the dead were commemorated.

Almost all savage races, like all nations in remote antiquity, regulate

---

* It is strange to mark how they were connected together. The dead were called Demetriakoi, or belonging to Ceres ; while the name of Proserpine means the bringer of fruits. They were evidently originally one Deity, presiding over the festival of agriculture and the dead. See Müller's History of the Dorians, translated by Sir Cornewall Lewis, II., 405.

† See as to the commencement of ancient year, Clinton's Fasti Hellenici, 355, 364, 366, 618.

‡ Greswell's Origines Kal. Ital. I, 429.

§ Hyde Rel. Vet. Pers., p. 230, 232, 248, 262.

## Haliburton *on the Festival of the Dead.*

their months by the new or the full moon, and hold festivals of a funereal character at the time of the new moon, or when the nights are darkest.

The Australians not only hold an annual corroboree of the Pleiades, but also a monthly corroboree of the moon, of three days duration, and apparently connected with a dread of ghosts, or a worship of the dead. They regulate their months by the full moon. The Hindoos offer in every lunar month, on Mahacala, the day of the conjunction, and defined as "*the day of the nearest approach to the sun*, obsequies to the manes of the *pitris*, or certain progenitors of the human race, to whom the *darker* fortnight is *peculiarly sacred.*" Sir William Jones, also says, referring to a Hindu work, "many subtle points are discussed by my author concerning *the junction of two*, or even *three lunar days in forming one fast or festival.*"*

The Chinese, the Africans, the Caribs, and other races of America, the Greeks, the Romans, and almost all ancient nations, kept a commemoration of the dead in the dark nights of the moon.†

Here we have an explanation for a monthly commemoration of the dead ; but why were the 17th, 18th and 19th days of each month, among some races, especially of a funereal character? Ellis tells us that the Society Islanders regard the 17th, 18th and 19th nights, as seasons "when spirits wander more than at any other time,"‡ a plain proof that even among the Pacific Islanders, these three days, in every month, must have been consecrated to the dead, as to this day, it is still believed in Britain, that on Halloween, when the festival of the dead once commenced, "the spirits of the dead wander more than at other times of the year." "This is a night when devils, witches, and other mischief making beings, are all abroad on their baleful midnight errands."

But the question arises, how came the beginning of the year to be, among some nations, on the 17th day of the month? The explanation, I think, is plain. The Chinese, the Hebrews, and other races, regulated the beginning of the year at the time of the new moon, *i. e.*, at the time of the festival held in the dark nights of the moon. With many races, the 17th, 18th, and 19th days after the full moon, or the three succeeding the new moon, or month, were evidently regarded as peculiarly sacred

* Sir William Jones' Works, (ed. 1807) vol. IV. p. 129.
† De Rougemont Le Peuple Primitif, 2, 246, 263, 355. Boulanger, I, 269 to 297 301. Horace, Odes III. 23.
‡ Ellis' Polynesean researches, I, 88. Ellis is evidently in error, in making the month commence at the new moon. If the Society Islanders commenced the month at the new moon, the nights peculiarly consecrated to the dead, would be the light nights, instead of the dark nights of the moon. If their month was like that of the Australians, the Hindoos, and other races, the 17th, 18th and 19th, would be the three dark nights succeeding the new moon, and would correspond with those devoted in Hindostan, and other countries, to a commemoration of the dead.

## Haliburton *on the Festival of the Dead.*

to the dead, and were the monthly days of rest, or the monthly *Sabbath* of heathen races.

Our own mode of regulating Easter, will serve to explain the commencement of the ancient year. The common prayer-book says : " Easter day is always the first Sunday after the full moon which happens upon or next after the 21st day of March." But the Hebrews substituted four sabbaths in place of one monthly time of rest, and used the vernal equinox, instead of the rising of the Pleiades, to regulate their Passover. Let us substitute the monthly festival of the dead for the word sabbath, and the rising of the Pleiades for the 21st March, and we read, " New Year's day is always the monthly sabbath after the full moon which happens upon or next after the culmination of the Pleiades at midnight." But as this would occur near the month of November, we can understand that when the months commencing with the full moon ceased to be lunar, and their festivals "moveable," the new year would, for some time at least, continue to commence on the 17th day of November, and that the 17th, 18th and 19th days of every month would still appear in ancient calendars as funereal days. We can also understand that a traditionary veneration for the 17th day of the month, especially of November, would long continue, like some old sea margin, to show the changes which time had effected ; and that the new year's festival of the dead, preserved in the mysteries of Isis and of Proserpine, would long be held on the 17th, 18th and 19th nights of the first month, though no longer those dark nights of the moon in which the spirits of the dead are wont to wander forth from their Maraes and their temples to receive the offerings of their trembling worshippers.*

Among the Romans we find a trace of a partial observance of the festival of the dead in November.† With the Northern year, commencing in February, the Romans borrowed from the Athenians their new year's festivals of the dead, the popular Anthesteria, and the mystic Eleusinian mysteries. The more ancient institution was the Lemuria, or festival of the ghosts, celebrated in May—a month, therefore, so unlucky that no marriage took place in it. Ovid and Greswell both agree as to the antiquity of the Lemuria. It is evident that this festival, transferred from November to May, was originally regulated by the heliacal rising of the Pleiades in the morning. Yet the offering to the spirits took place at

---

* This view is confirmed by a festival of Callee, the Hindoo Isis, taking place at the new moon after the full moon of November.

Wherever we find the festivals of a nation, especially those of a mournful or funereal character, occurring on the 15th or on the 17th, 18th and 19th days of the month, there is strong reason to assume that the month must have originally commenced, not with the new, but with the full moon. Among the Hindoos, both systems are in vogue. See on this point Greswell's Fasti Catholici, I. 62. Sir William Jones' works, IV. 128.

† Sauberti de Sacrificiis, 89.

## Haliburton *on the Festival of the Dead.*

midnight, a time when that constellation was invisible. What can have made that hour so peculiarly marked ?

> "Non haec Pleiades faciunt, nec aquosus Orion."*

Greswell connects this circumstance with the November festival of the Aztecs, which commenced in the evening, and in which midnight was the hour of sacrifice.  On this he constructs a theory as to their festival commemorating the event of the sun having gone back ten degrees in the days of Hezekiah.  His remarks as to the Aztec festival, supply a clue to the fact, that the Lemuria must have been moved from November to May, from the month when the Pleiades rose in the evening and culminated at midnight, to May when they were invisible till early dawn ; and above all, they will prove that a miracle should be the *dernier ressort* of a philosopher, and that he should be the last to consider "omne ignotum pro mirifico."†

Before concluding this necessarily superficial sketch of this primeval new year's festival, a subject respecting which scores of volumes might be written, I must turn to Britain to see if we have among us any traces of this primitive year, or seasons of the Pleiades.  That it did exist among the Celtic race‡ has long been known to those who have studied its history and customs.  Wylde says " the first great division of the year was into summer and winter, Samradh and Geimradh, the former beginning in May, or Bealtine, and the latter in November, or Samhfhuim, summer end.  On the first of May took place the great Druid festival of Beal or Bel, and at the beginning of November All Halloween ;§ and it is strange

---

° Propertius II, 16, 51.

† " The ceremony of the secular fire among the Aztecs, the oldest, the most solemn, and most sacred of all in their calendar, seems to imply the same thing of them ; for that was celebrated at midnight ; that is though the ceremony itself *began at sunset*, the consummation or conclusion, by the lighting anew of the secular fire, took place *at midnight*. The primitive rule of the cycle," (the noctidiurnal system, the day commencing in the evening,) " and a co-ordinate rule borrowed from midnight, seem both to have been associated in this one ceremony.

" We have very little doubt indeed that, were the truth known, both the ceremony of the secular fire, and the change of the rule of the noctidiurnal cycle (if it must be so called) among these nations, would be found to be ultimately due to the miracle of B. C. 710, and to the circumstance under which it took place among them, and to the effect which it produced on their fears and apprehensions."  But the connection of the Pleiades with the Aztec festival, seems to have somewhat puzzled Greswell.  " We recommend this point to the notice of astronomers.  The fact is certain that the culmination of this particular constellation, was one of the phenomena presented by the heavens, to which the Aztecs in particular, for some reason or other, looked with peculiar interest, and attached peculiar importance.  It was associated with the ceremony of the secular fire, and apparently from the first ; the moment prescribed for the offering of the stated sacrifice, followed by the rekindling of the extinguished fires, being precisely that when the Pleiades were in the middle of the sky.  What, too, was so likely to give occasion to a ceremony of this kind (the extinction of fires of every kind at a stated time), as the sudden extinction of the light of the sun itself in the midst of its meridian splendor."— Fasti Catholici I, 362 ; as to Lemuria, p. 356 ; also see risings of stars being reversed, p. 343.

‡ Wylde's Irish Popular Superstitions, p. 38.

§ That Halloween was not only a funereal, but also an agricultural festival, is perfectly clear. Associated in Britain with a harvest home, the *Kernbaby*, or Cornbaby, must have once been one of its features.  The following passage is in point:

Shaw, in his History of the Province of Moray, p. 241, says " A solemnity was kept on the eve of the 1st November, as *a thanks giving for the safe ingathering of the produce of the fields.* This, I am told, but have not seen it, is observed in Buchan, and other Counties, by having *Hallow eve fires* kindled on some rising ground." Brand's Pop. Ant. 388.

## Haliburton *on the Festival of the Dead.*

that both the eve of May day, and Halloween, are ill-omened nights, on which prudent persons in Ireland, from fear of encountering fairies and ghosts, avoid being out after dark.*

Classical writers of antiquity tell us that in Britain Ceres and Proserpine were worshipped in the same manner as in the mysteries of the Cabiri. Now we have seen that Proserpine and her mother Ceres are really the same Deities, both being connected with agriculture and the dead. In Sicily, Ceres was worshipped in May, and Proserpine in the autumn.† The latter was called Core, or the damsel. Are there any traces of her still in Britain? It is manifest that the May queen, and the Kernbaby of the harvest home, are either relics of this deity, or the origin of the myth. But we have evidence that they are as old, if not older than Proserpine herself. In the Tonga Islands, at a first fruits celebration, a child presides as a sort of Southern queen of the spring, a November queen, if I may give her a new title.

The Tow Tow, a species of first fruits celebration, takes place " at the time when the yams are approaching maturity, *in the early part of November*," when prayers are offered up to A'lo A'lo, the God of weather. Mariner, in describing it, says " a deputation of nine or ten men from the priests of A'lo A'lo, all dressed in mats, with green leaves round their necks, arrives with a female child, to represent the wife of A'lo A'lo".‡ They offer up a prayer for a fruitful season to the god, and then divide the provisions collected for the occasion. One pile being assigned to A'lo A'lo, and to other gods. Mariner tells us that " she is selected from the chiefs of the higher ranks, and *is about eight or ten years old ;* during the eighty days of this ceremony, she resides at the consecrated house of A'lo A'lo, where, a day before the ceremony, a cava party is held, at which she presides, as well as at a feast which follows. She has nothing to do on the actual days of the ceremony, except to come with the deputation and to sit down with them." Here then we have, South of the Equator, a " queen of the May," or a *Kernbaby*, whichever we may call her. But in China, Core, or the damsel, assumes more distinctly the funereal cha-

---

○ See Wylde, 52 to 58 ; Brady's Clavis Calendaria ; also, Brand's Popr. Antiquities, v. I, p. 390.

† This festival is such a conclusive proof of the myth having reference to the two seasons of the Pleiades, that I cannot omit mention of it. In the autumn, for three days, Ceres mourns for her daughter, who, for six months, is visible on earth, and for the rest of the year is compelled to reign with Pluto in hell. Now, it is manifest that she was invisible from May to November, because after three days' search in November, she rises to light once more, and is received with great rejoicings. But this is the very time of the year when the great festival " of the Pleiads above" is celebrated by the Australians. The fact that there was a temple in Sicily,○ in which Ceres or Proserpine, and the Pleiades were jointly worshipped, confirms my view of this strange myth.
○ See Dupuis, V. 270.

‡ Mariner's Tonga Islands, 385.

## Haliburton *on the Festival of the Dead.*

racter of Proserpine.* At the festival of the dead, a child presides, who receives the offerings made to deceased ancestors.† In the South she is the wife of A'lo, the god of weather, but in Grecian mythology, she is "in autumn wed"‡ to Pluto, the god of the dead; and in Egyptian fables, she is doomed, at the November festival of the new year, to mourn Osiris, the God of Agriculture and "the Lord of Tombs." It would be strange, if, in the half naked little Fiji savage, the wife of A'lo, we should find a clue to her, who was "the ancient goddess" in the days of the Patriarchs, and whose statues bore the inscription, "I am all that has been, that shall be; and none among mortals has hitherto taken off my veil."§

Such then, north of the Equator, are the scattered fragments of, what

* Since writing the above, I have met with a very interesting confirmation of my views Callee,'the Hindoo Core, "who appears," says Sir William Jones, "in the *calijug, as a damsel twelve years old*," presides over a festival of the dead at the beginning of October. "She wore a necklace of golden skulls descriptive of the dreadful rites in which she took so gloomy a delight." The offerings which were prescribed by the Vedas were human sacrifices, for which, however, bulls and horses were substituted. Soul cakes are also consecrated to her, as they were to Proserpine in Greece, as the deity presiding over the dead.
Our soldiers found at Cawnpore an ode invoking "the black Goddess," the cruel Callee, written by Nina Sahib before the outbreak. The soul cake, the symbol of revolt among the Hindoos, was the emblem of this bloody goddess; and there can be but little doubt that the slaughter of our unhappy countrymen was regarded by the fanatical Sepoys as a welcome offering to their sanguinary deity. If any of her victims had ever in their native land been at a rustic "maying," or harvest home, how little could they have dreamed, as they looked at the May Queen or the Kernbaby, that they saw before them the primitive type of a cruel deity, at whose altar they were doomed to be sacrificed!—See Sir William Jones' works IV. 185.—Maurice's Indian antiquities, II. 181. Hardwicke, the late Christian Advocate at Cambridge, is strangely in error on this point; see "Christ and our other Masters," part II, page 19.—See as to worship of the dead, III, 32, 195, 176, 196, IV, 78.
† De Rougemont, Peuple Primitive," v. II, p. 356.
‡ See Orphic Hymn to Proserpine.
§ Exhibiting a funereal and agricultural character, the ancient mysteries were, as we have seen, clearly connected, by their very time of observance, with the new year's celebration of the South, the festival of first fruits, and of the dead. But even their obscene rites and their peculiar secrecy, may be solved by a reference to the savages of Australia and of Central Africa. Europeans, who have been initiated by the Australians into their mysteries, which they describe as being of an obscene nature, whenever they make themselves known to the natives by the secret signs they have learned, are implored not to divulge the sacred mysteries.
The same freemasonry exists among the natives of America, and of Central Africa. Among the latter the priest is called an *Obi* man, and the temples where these secret rites are observed are called *Oboni*, or houses of *Obi*, and are ornamented with phallic emblems, or symbols of generation.
Now, I have found, that *Obi* means, in Central Africa, *an ancestor*, one who begets. Hence the Obi man is inspired by ancestors, and the Oboni are temples of the dead. Our very word necromancy (prophecying by aid of the dead) carries us back to the Obi of the Africans. At the Oracle of Delphi, the priestess, before she uttered responses, was inspired by Ob, and must have been originally nothing more or less than an Obi woman.
Is it not strange that phallic emblems, though so very offensively significant, have been assigned by the learned to almost everything except the worship of ancestors?—See Report on Aborigines, p. 64, 69, 76.—See Bowen's Central Africa, (New York, 1857,) p. 271, 315 to 319; also Dictionary of Yoruba Language, Smithsonian Contributions, X., xvi. xix. 109.—De Rougemont's Peuple Primitif, II, 363. I refer those who may take an interest in such matters, to the following authorities as to the funereal character of ancient mysteries, and the time of their observance, &c.: Dupuis 1., 264, and seq., 312, 340, 349, 364, 390, 402, 410, 422, 427, 439, 443. Boulanger L'antiquite devoilee, 1., p. 269 to 308; III., 178 to 186. St. Croix sur les Mysteres du Paganisme, I. 54, 55, 66, 75, 78, 817, 340, et passim. Le Monde Primitif, III. 339. Ouvaroff on the Mysteries, p. 1, 27; also Christie's notes, 169, 172. Warburton's Divine Legation of Moses, Faber's Origin of Pagan Idolatry, and Bryant's Mythology, are principally devoted to a subject, which has caused more learned and fruitless speculation than any other topic connected with the history of ancient nations.

## Haliburton *on the Festival of the Dead.*

we can only regard as the wreck of the primitive Southern year, and of its New Year's festival of first fruits, and the dead. I have endeavoured to collect together these *disjecti membra*, diffused and hitherto lost in vague myths, confused calendars, uncertain traditions, and obsolete customs.* Yet, in the New, as well as in the Old World, civilized and savage races gaze with equal wonder on the memorials, that everywhere exist, of the observance of this festival by primeval man. In the large deposits of ashes, and of the remains of food, found in vast burial tumuli in Australia, America and Asia, the graves of races long extinct,† we have significant evidence of this new year's commemoration dating back to the most remote ages; while even at the burial cave at Aurignac, to which an antiquity of not less than 8000 years is assigned by some authorities, we have the same memorials of the feasts and fires of this ancient festival.‡ Its memory has long been forgotten. Preserved only in the rites of heathen races, or merely lingering, among civilized nations, in the customs and superstitions of the peasantry, this festival has never been considered worthy of the attention of the historian or of the ethnologist; and

* Though it has required much time and labor to collect even the materials which I have used, respecting this festival north of the equator, the difficulty has been far greater in obtaining any definite information regarding its observance in the southern hemisphere; first, because travellers are generally ignorant of, or inattentive to the festivals of savage races, and rarely specify the time or the particulars of their observance; and secondly, because in a colony, from the absence of extensive libraries, it is almost impossible to glean precise information, which, even if it exists, can only be procured from a large number of writers. As regards Polynesia, I have felt this difficulty very much. Ellis, on whom I have had mainly to rely, though he regards the Polynesians as belonging to the same race, and almost identical in their customs and religious ideas, does not clear up a point of no little importance in these investigations, as to the festival of the dead, and the year of the Pleiades existing universally throughout the Pacific Islands, his remarks being, in a great measure, confined to the groups of numerous Islands, known as the Georgian, and Society Islands. Even his work I could not procure while writing this paper. I had therefore to rely on notes made some years ago, while reading his works, before my attention had been particularly drawn to this subject. As, however, south of the equator, on the west coast of South America, among the ancient Peruvians, as well as in the southern Pacific, in Tahiti, the Tonga Islands, and Australia, we find the year of the Pleiades or its New Year's festival, there can be but little doubt that equally distinct traces of them will be found in the more northern islands of the Pacific. A reference to Crawford's "Indian Archipelago" will confirm this view. See I., 28.

† See Report on Aborigines, p. 62. The work of Messrs. Squier and Davis on the Mississippi mounds, and Dr. McPherson's researches at Kertch, throw a light on this subject.

‡ The existence of articles resembling American wampum in the cave at Aurignac, is peculiarly interesting, both as tending to throw light on the habits of the race that then existed in Europe, and as giving some clue to their representatives among existing nations. The cowrie (Cyprea moneta) is used in Asia and Africa, and is entirely different from the relics to which I refer. In America, shell money is made from the shell of the hard shelled clam, (mercenaria violacea, Schum.) which is cut into small oblong pieces, perforated for the purpose of being strung into "*belts* of wampum," which are buried with the possessor at his death. Hence in most Indian graves we find numerous pieces of perforated shell. This throws a light on the following passage in Sir Charles Lyell's "Antiquity of man," (p. 188.) "Mixed with the human bones, inside the grotto, first removed by Bonnemaison, were eighteen small, round and flat plates of a white, shelly substance, made of some species of Cockle (cardium), and pierced through the middle, as if for being strung into a bracelet."

As there is no further remark made concerning these specimens resembling wampum, soon after the work appeared, I drew the author's attention to the point. They are plainly not cowries, as the shape precludes such an inference.

Should the use of wampum be limited to the New World, an inquiry into this subject may lead to interesting conclusions. The mode of making wampum is described in a note to "Rule and Misrule of the English in America," by the author of Sam Slick, b. ii., ch. v. See Prehistoric Man. by Dr. Danl. Wilson, I, 218, 443, II. 147.

## Haliburton *on the Festival of the Dead.*

this paper is the first attempt that has been made to throw any light on its history or its origin.

I have restricted my remarks to such points as connect it with a year commencing in November, a branch in itself far too extensive for the space at my disposal. My next paper will show the light which this festival, occurring in February, throws on the primitive northern year; and my third will be devoted to a far more interesting and easier branch of enquiry, as to the prime origin of this festival of the dead, and the influence it has exerted on the idolatry, the mythology, and the religious rites of all ancient nations, an influence even still descernable in the customs and modes of thought of civilized nations.

That, from Australia to Britain, we have all inherited this primitive year and its new year's festival, from a common source, is plainly manifest. Was it carried south by northern nations; or, has there been a migration of southern races to northern latitudes?

That the " Feast of Ancestors," which still lingers in our All Halloween, All Saints and All Souls, is the same as the *Inachi* of the South, and was originally the New Year's festival of a primitive year commencing in November, is a matter, which can, I believe, be established beyond any question; but in what part of the world it first originated, is necessarily, with me, a matter of vague conjecture only, especially with the limited materials I possess respecting the festivals of southern races. The fact, that the year of the Pleiades, as well as the ancient reverence for that constellation, only now exists south of the equator, is, however, in itself very significant.

We have hitherto examined the universal customs of nations, let us now turn to those wide spread primitive traditions, which, though hitherto unexplained, and apparently inconsistent with each other, have been regarded from the days of Plato to the present, as embodying the dim outlines of primeval history.

First—We have the very remarkable tradition of remote antiquity, referred to by Plato, and by modern writers, as to the sun, moon and stars having once risen in the opposite quarter to what they now do. Greswell* regards the tradition as historical evidence of a miracle. Can it be explained by natural causes? It can; but only in one way—by supposing a migration of races from south to north of the equator.

To the Tahitians, the sun, moon and stars rise on their right hand; to us, they rise on our left.

* Fasti Catholici I, 343.

## Haliburton *on the Festival of the Dead.*

Second—The most ancient tradition perhaps in the world, one that has left its impress on the astronomical systems, the religious rites, and even the social customs of nations from Syria to Japan, preserves the belief of the Chaldæans that the first inhabitants of Asia were a maritime race that landed on the shores of the Persian gulf.*

Third—From China to ancient Britain prevailed the uniform belief that the ancestors of the human race came from Islands; and from the time of Plato to the present, scores of volumes have been. written on the subject.† A celebrated French philosopher asks us, "Ne trouvez vous pas, Monsieur, quelque chose de singulier, dans cet amour des anciens pour les isles ? Tout ce qu'il y a de sacré, de grand, et d'antique, s'y est passé : pourquoi les habitans du continent ont ils donné cet avantage aux isles, sur le continent même ?"‡ An enthusiastic Welshman has gone near home for the primeval paradise, though a mistaken impression undoubtedly existed among ancient nations, that Britain much more nearly resembled the infernal regions.§

Let us imagine that a migration did take place from Southern latitudes, and what would be the result ? The wanderers would bear with them a recollection of the Islands of the south, which they had left. They would see with dread, and remember long, that the stars that once rose on their right hand, had apparently reversed their movements. They might bring with them a year of seasons only suited to their former homes. The stars that once announced spring would long continue to be reverenced as the Vergiliæ, though rising at the beginning of summer. Once marking the commencement of the year by appearing to their worshippers on the southern Halloween, and hence causing " the evening and the morning" to be "the first day," the Pleiades would long retain their name as the Hesperides (the stars of the evening), even when they had ceased to regulate the year, when their "pleasant influences" had been forgotten ; when their rising in the evening was no longer reverenced, and their heliacal rising and setting in the morning was alone regarded ;‖ when even that mode of regulating the seasons, had become disused, and the past influence and history of the Pleiads only existed as a matter of fable, and of doubt even to Astronomers themselves.

* Faber's, II. 378, De Rongemont, I. 325. Dupais, V. 1. Layard's Nineveh and its remains II. 466.
† De Rougement, II. 248. Faber's origin of Pagan idolatry, 1. 393.
‡ Letters sur L'Atlantide, par M. Bailly, p. 361.
§ Davies' Mythology of the British Druids, 158, 181.
‖ See Greswell's Orig. Kal. Ital. III. 58, 460, 516. Also, Fasti Catholici, II. 110, which is part cularly in point, also 104. Dupuis IX, 183. Sir Cornewall Lewis' Astronomy of the Ancients, p. 11, 25, 60 to 67.

## Haliburton *on the Festival of the Dead.*

Yet we find among ancient nations, that the Hesperides were connected most singularly with the traditions as to the primitive abodes of our race. The Southern Garden of the Hesperides recalls them to our mind;* while the name of these daughters of Atlas and of the Ocean, is blended with the memory of the lost Island of Atlantis. The key to many a mysterious myth will yet be found in the history of the seasons of the Pleiades.†

It is not less interesting to mark the wreck of the southern year, and of its New Year's festival of first fruits and of the dead, over which the Virgiliæ once presided.

In some cases, as in ancient Egypt, in Britain and Persia, we find it stranded in November as an ancient popular observance, though the year had long ceased to commence in that month. In other countries it drifted off from the autumn to form a New Year's festival in February. In one instance it shared the fate of the Pleiades, and took place, as the Lemuria of the Romans, in May, in which month it must have once been regulated by the heliacal rising of the *Hesperides* in the *morning ;* while the year of two seasons only survived in fables as to the two-faced Janus, or as matters of doubt and mystery to astronomers.

So entirely have the history and "the pleasant influences of the Pleiades" been forgotten, that the latest work on the astronomy of the ancients does not even refer to the primitive year commencing in November, or to the Pleiades as dividing its seasons. Even where history has

* See Dupuis I, 329. De Rougemont, II, 248.
† As the fables of Io and Icarus, hitherto unexplained, seem to relate to traditions as to a migration of races, and to changes in the seasons, it may be worth while to refer to them here. Io, the daughter of *Inachus*, is the same as Isis, who, we have seen, is plainly a mythical embodiment of the primitive year, and of its funereal and agricultural New Year's festival. The name of the Hindoo Isis, Call, means *time*. Mythology tells us that Io, accompanied by the Pleiades, after wandering over the whole earth, and being persecuted by Juno, on account of Jupiter, arrived at last at the Nile, where she was worshipped as Isis. To what can this refer, except to a year regulated by the Pleiades, having been brought from some distant country, and embodied in the myth of Isis. The fable of Io appears plainly in the Hindoo god, *Carticeya*, (the Pleiades?). A reference to the representation of him, given by Sir Wm. Jones, will leave but little doubt on this point. By his name, as well as by his crown of seven stars, he represents the Pleiades. By his faces looking in opposite directions, and by his six arms on each side, Janus bifrons, and the year of two seasons of six months each ; while in the peacock, on which he rides, we have the well known classical emblem of the many eyed Argus, the watchful keeper of Io.
Sir William Jones calls Carticeya the Hindoo Orus ; but Orus or Horus, Bunsen says, unites in himself all the myths of Isis and Osiris.
The persecutions of Io, probably refer *to* traditions, as to the seasons having changed, in consequence of a migration of races, and having become unsuited to the year and its festivals.
Icarus falling short in his flight, from Jupiter or the sun having melted the wax with which his wings were fastened on, must also have reference to a change in the time of harvest.
Now it is a curious coincidence, if nothing more, that in Africa, to this day, *Oro* is still worshipped, as he is in Polynesia. *Ixi* means a new period of time, *tximi* a feast or festival, and *ikore the harvest.*
See Sir Wm. Jones' works III, p. 363.
Bunsen's Egypt's Place in Universal History, I. 434 to 437.
Dicty. of Yoruba Language—introd. XVII.
Bowen's Central Africa, p. 272, 317.
The learned have invariably ignored the fact, that Greek mythology points, with singular uniformity, not to Egypt or to Asia for its origin, but to Ethiopia, and the ocean beyond Africa.

## Haliburton *on the Festival of the Dead.*

preserved the tale of the Aztecs regulating their cycle in November by the culmination of the Pleiades, Greswell considers the circumstance so remarkable, as to deserve the special attention of Astronomers, and assumes that, if explained, it will favor his view as to there having been once a miraculous suspension of the laws that govern the universe.

It is not gratifying, it is true, for civilized and refined nations to trace their origin to the savages of the Pacific Islands, yet those persons who may dislike the conclusion to which this enquiry tends, may, if they agree in the correctness of my views, console themselves by remembering the monuments of an extinct civilization, that are still to be found in those Islands, and that must have been the work of races far superior to the present natives of Polynesia.*

Yet the Islands of the southern ocean most nearly realize the memory of the Fortunate Isles, "where the air was wholesome and temperate, and the earth produced an immense number of fruits, without the labors of men." The early European voyagers, transported with the beauty and salubrity of the Islands of the Pacific, fixed upon them as the primeval abodes of our race. Even nature would appear to confirm the impression. There the very ocean and the stars seem subservient to man. The tides with unvarying regularity† mark morning and evening, midday and midnight; the Pleiades divide the seasons and regulate the year; and "the celestial clock,"‡ the brilliant Southern Cross, by its deflection in the heavens, proclaims the hours of the night.

The conclusions to which ethology§ has led me, that we must look south of the equator, if we would find the origin of our November festival of the dead, or a solution for the traditions as to the Pleiades, receive a very significant confirmation from the following passage in a lecture

---

° I refer here to the singular remains in the Easter Islands, that have attracted so much attention.—Ellis' Pol. Res., III. 325.

† "But the most remarkable circumstance is the uniformity of the time of high and low water. During the year, whatever be the age or situation of the moon, the water is lowest at six in the morning, and at the same hour in the evening, and highest at noon, and midnight. This is so well established, that the time of night is marked by the ebbing and flowing of the tide; and in all the Islands, the term for high water and midnight is the same."—Polynesian Res. I. 29.

‡ Humbolt's Cosmos, translated by O. C. Otte, (N.Y. 1850) II. 290.

§ I may, I trust, be pardoned for coining a new word for researches into a subject hitherto considered to be either unworthy of attention or closed against regular investigation. That the customs and superstitions of nations are most wonderfully enduring memorials of the past, will, I trust, be apparent from some of the facts contained in this paper. When I come to treat more particularly of the festival of the dead and of its origin, this will be much more conclusively established. Even should the interpretations, which I have given, prove entirely incorrect, it will be plain that, to more competent enquirers, the study of customs opens up a new and most interesting field, that is even more susceptible of scientific research, and that will shed more light on the social and religious life of primitive man, than philology itself.

The Father of History says, "Pindar appears to me to have truly said that custom is the king of all men;" and Sir William Jones, the only modern writer, who seems to have duly

## Appendix Two

*Primitive Astronomical Traditions as to Paradise.*
*By* R. G. HALIBURTON

The author had met with a great mass of primitive legends among savages as to a primaeval paradise, with its Tree of Life and of Knowledge, being situated in the stars of Taurus, the Pleiades. As far back as 1863 he privately printed a paper entitled' New Materials for the History of Man, derived from a comparison of the Calendars and Festivals of Nations.'

In the course of these astronomical researches, he had met, to his surprise, with curious traditions as to a Paradise and deluge, the cross, a tree or bough, and a bird connected with the primitive year and its festivals.

He had since devoted much careful study to this enigma, and the present paper gave only a portion of these investigations, for the subject was too wide to be outlined in a paper.

Half a century ago, many learned works were devoted to coincidences in the religious ideas, traditions, and symbols of nations; and it was by some supposed that they were distorted vestiges of the sacred narrative, but this view had been abandoned, and all these learned investigations had been discredited.

We now cut the Gordian knot, which we cannot solve, as to these common traditions and beliefs, and suppose them of indigenous growth. But, while this conclusion might, in many instances, be right, there were many coincidences too arbitrary and widely spread to admit of the solution that the beliefs and religious ideas of primitive races were all the emanations of darkness, stagnation, and decay.

The author then selected some American traditions as to the Tree of Life and Paradise.

The symbols of a cross and a bough or tree, he thought, were suggested by the form of the Pleiades, which when they set have a remarkable resemblance to a prostrate tree.

The Kiowas of the prairies believe that in the shape of the Pleiades and of some adjoining stars can be seen the form of their great lather in Heaven, the great Kiowa.

Once upon a time he went far to the West and met with a prostrate tree or trunk which he struck three times. At the first stroke human beings of misshapen, monstrous forms came forth. These he put to rights, placed them back in the tree and struck it a second time, when perfect men and women came forth from this tree of life.

He placed them again in the tree, and struck it a third time, when men and women and children that had been born, came out of it. He instructed the men and women in the rude arts of savage life, and then went up to the Pleiades.

This belief in our having sprung from a tree is well known in the Old World, in Britain, Lapland, Germany, Greece, Persia, and other countries.

An Indian tribe of the Pampas, the Abipones, believe that their Great Father resides in the Pleiades, and when these stars disappear from the heavens for a time, it is believed that he dies or is ill, and when those stars reappear his revival is hailed with joy. This gives a clue to the death and revival of the gods of antiquity.

These people use the symbol of those' stars of rain,' the prehistoric cross, as an ornament or sacred sign.

There is also a, curious tradition of seven giant brothers, who fished off the west coast of Canada. They struck a huge monster with a harpoon.

As the rope could not be loosened, they were dragged far into the ocean towards a vast whirlpool.

Just as they neared it, the rope broke, and they sailed up to the Pleiades, where they are now visible as the seven stars.

These seven brothers give us a clue to the seven Cabeiric brothers, of Phoenician tradition, who sailed in the first ship, and who have been identified with the Pleiades by Movers.

But the story of the whirlpool is especially important, for we meet it in the traditions of the Dyaks of Borneo, some of the ancestors of whom, as they were sailing in a boat, saw near a great waterfall the boughs of a tree touching the waters, and loaded with fruit.

A Dyak climbed up the tree to see where its roots grew. He found out the enigma which is described in the Song of Odin, who hung nine days from a mystic tree,' of which no one knows where its roots grow.'

The Dyak reached a heavenly country,' the land of the Pleiades, where he was taught agriculture, and other arts, by a kind being who dwells there, and then, bringing with him from the Pleiades the gift of rice or corn, he was let down by a rope from the seven stars, and imparted to his countrymen the mystic lore which he bad learned by climbing that tree of knowledge.'

This waterfall recalls the waterfall of the river Styx, and the whirlpool of the Haida tradition; also the whirlpool of Scylla and Charybdis, over which hung a great fig tree.

A great number of interesting points were adduced connecting the primitive traditions of the natives of America and Polynesia with those of the Old World.

The three Graces were, among the Iroquois, three loving sisters in the Pleiades, the spirits of the bean, the squash, and maize, their gifts to mortals.

They are called' Our Life, our Supporters'—the very words addressed to the spirit of agriculture in Mexico, and to this day in the Atlas country.

The Lycian women of old invoked the bull to come and bring the Graces with him; and the bull of the mysteries is represented with the three Graces on its head, and the Pleiades following them.

This referred to the constellation Taurus, or the bull, in which the Pleiades were placed. When' the bull with its white horns opened the year,' it brought, all over the world, a kindly New Year's feast of family love.

Even among the head-hunting Dyaks of Borneo, Bishop Chalmers was asked on New Year's Day to go out to the assembled people and to give them his wishes for a happy New Year.

In many parts of the world it is followed by visits, gifts, and good wishes. This is one of the oldest and most universal festivals.

## Bibliography

"Ancient and Modern Physics: An Enquiry. (Concluded.)."
*The Theosophical Forum* 10.12 (1905): 222. Print.

"Billy Meier." *Wikipedia*. N.p., 29 Oct. 2010. Web. 29 Oct.
2010. <http://en.wikipedia.org/wiki/Billy_Meier>.

Blavatsky, Helena Petrovna, and George Stow Mead. *The
Theosophical Glossary*. London: Theosophical
Publishing Society, 1892. Print.

Blavatsky Lodge of Theosophists. "The Pleiades (from the
Secret Doctrine)." *Theosophical outlook* 3-4 (1918):
71, 209, 411-412. Print.

Butler, Hiram E. "Editorial." *The Esoteric* 4 (1891): 250.
Print.

Camp, F. M. G. "Our Pygmy Brothers." *Universal
brotherhood - Volume 13* Nov. 1898: 429. Print.

"Cherokee Serpent Prophecy." *Starseed - Tribe.net*. N.p., n.d.
Web. 1 Nov. 2010.
<http://starseed.tribe.net/thread/1bab5303-7bfa-
45a1-9ec3-e6fb72988e6a>.

Clark, James Albert. *A theosophist's point of view*. District of
Columbia: Press of the Pathfinder, 1901. Print.

Clow, Barbara Hand. "Journeys Through Nine Dimensions."

    *Hand Clow 2012*. N.p., n.d. Web. 1 Nov. 2010.

    <http://www.handclow2012.com/pleiadianagenda.h

    tm>.

"Elizabeth Klarer." *Wikipedia*. N.p., 25 Oct. 2010. Web. 29

    Oct. 2010.

    <http://en.wikipedia.org/wiki/Elizabeth_Klarer>.

Erickson, Einar C. "The Dead Sea Scrolls -- Possible Parallels

    to Mormon Doctrine and Practices ." *Ancient*

    *Mormon Doctrine Scholar Dr. Einar C. Erickson*.

    N.p., 12 July 2006. Web. 4 Nov. 2010.

    <http://www.einarerickson.com/content/view/12/3

    8/1/9/>.

"Francis Crick." *Wikipedia*. N.p., 29 Oct. 2010. Web. 1 Nov.

    2010.

    <http://en.wikipedia.org/wiki/Francis_Crick>.

Haliburton, R. G. "Haliburton on the Festival of the Dead."

    *Proceedings and transactions of the Nova Scotian*

    *Institute of Natural Science* 1 (1867): 61-84. Print.

Hastings, James, et al. *A Dictionary of the Bible: Kir-*

    *Pleiades*. New York City: Charles Scribner's Sons,

    1900. Print.

Herzog, Johann Jakob, Philip Schaff, and Albert Hauck. *The new Schaff-Herzog encyclopedia of religious knowledge: embracing Biblical, historical, doctrinal, and practical theology and Biblical, theological, and ecclesiastical biography from the earliest times to the present day, Volume 11*. New York: Funk and Wagnalls Company, 1911. Print.

Hewitt, James Francis. *The ruling races of prehistoric times in India, southwestern Asia, and southern Europe, Volume 1*. London: Archibald Constable and Company, 1884. Print.

"Howard Menger." *Wikipedia*. N.p., 11 Oct. 2010. Web. 29 Oct. 2010. <http://en.wikipedia.org/wiki/Howard_Menger>.

Jiang, Peter, and Jenny Li. "Research findings continues work of DNA Nobel Prize Winner Dr. Francis Crick." *Biblioteca Pleyades*. N.p., 26 Jan. 2007. Web. 4 Nov. 2010. <http://www.bibliotecapleyades.net/ciencia/ciencia_adn08.htm>.

Judge, William Q. "Cyclic Impression and Return." *Theosophy* Jan. 18967: 307. Print.

Lowie, Robert H. "The test-theme in North American
mythology." *Journal of American Folk-Lore*.
Volume XXI ed. 1908. Print.

"Lyra." *Exopaedia*. N.p., n.d. Web. 1 Nov. 2010.
<http://www.exopaedia.org/display.php?by=topic&
val=Lyra>.

"Lyra: Mythology, Legends and Lore." *United Starseeds*.
Atlantis Rising, n.d. Web. 1 Nov. 2010.
<http://www.unitedstarseeds.org/group/LYRANSI
RIUS/forum/topics/lyra-mythology-legends-lore>.

"Lyran Starseeds." *United Starseeds*. Atlantis Rising, n.d.
Web. 1 Nov. 2010.
<http://www.unitedstarseeds.org/group/LYRANSI
RIUS?xg_source=activity>.

Marciniak, Barbara. *The Pleiadians with Barbara
Marciniak*. N.p., n.d. Web. 4 Nov. 2010.
<http://www.pleiadians.com/>.

"Maya Astronomy." *Authentic Maya*. N.p., 13 June 2010.
Web. 1 Nov. 2010.
<http://authenticmaya.com/maya_astronomy.htm>

McKnight, Lloyd. "Consciousness, The Self And The

Quantum World." *Facebook*. N.p., n.d. Web. 4 Nov.

2010. <http://te-

in.facebook.com/topic.php?uid=2494641105&topic

=3458&post=36174>.

"Messier Object 45." *SEDS: Students for the Exploration*

*and Development of Space*. N.p., 10 Mar. 2009.

Web. 29 Oct. 2010.

<http://www.seds.org/messier/m/m045.html>.

"Michael Salla." *Wikipedia*. N.p., 26 Oct. 2010. Web. 29 Oct.

2010.

<http://en.wikipedia.org/wiki/Michael_Salla>.

Moilliet, S. H. Keir. "Suggested parallel between the

pyramidal form and the growth of religion." *Broad*

*lines; or, The true theosophy*. 1890. Print.

Moody, J. Ward, and Michael D. Rhodes. "Astronomy and

the Creation in the Book of Abraham." *Neal A.*

*Maxwell Institute*. Brigham Young University, n.d.

Web. 4 Nov. 2010.

<http://maxwellinstitute.byu.edu/publications/boo

ks/?bookid=40&chapid=162>.

Mueller, Friedrich Max. *Theosophy or Psychological religion: the Gifford lectures delivered before the University of Glasgow in 1892*. London: Longmans, Green and co., 1893. Print.

Murdoch, Walter. *The Oxford Book of Australasian Verse*. London: Oxford University Press, 1918. Print.

"The names of the Watchers." *Ziarah.net*. N.p., n.d. Web. 2 Nov. 2010. <http://echoes.devin.com/watchers/names.html>.

"THE NEW WORLD ORDER: THE ALIEN CONNECTION (A Synopsis of the Good Guys and the Bad Guys in Space) ." *Biblioteca Pleyades*. N.p., 1993. Web. 4 Nov. 2010. <http://www.bibliotecapleyades.net/bb/draconis03.htm>.

Nibley, Hugh. "A Strange Thing in the Land: The Return of

the Book of Enoch, Part 1." *LDS.org - Ensign Article.*

Church of Jesus Christ of Latter-Day Saints, Oct.

1975. Web. 4 Nov. 2010.

<http://lds.org/ldsorg/v/index.jsp?hideNav=1&loca

le=0&sourceId=ed2661cb2b86b010VgnVCM10000

04d82620a_____&vgnextoid=2354fccf2b7db010Vgn

VCM1000004d82620aRCRD>.

"Nordic Aliens." *Wikipedia.* N.p., 27 Oct. 2010. Web. 29 Oct.

2010. <http://en.wikipedia.org/wiki/Pleiadeans>.

"144,000 Annointed - Something to think about...... Who is

their God? Where is he?" *MM Outreach Inc.* N.p.,

n.d. Web. 4 Nov. 2010.

<http://mmoutreachinc.com/jehovahs_witnesses/w

hichgod.html>.

"Orfeo Angelucci." *Wikipedia.* N.p., 29 Oct. 2010. Web. 29

Oct. 2010.

<http://en.wikipedia.org/wiki/Orfeo_Angelucci>.

Pember, George Hawkins. *Earth's earliest ages, and their

connection with modern spiritualism and

theosophy.* London: Hodder and Stoughton, 1884.

Print.

"Pleiades." *Exopaedia*. N.p., n.d. Web. 1 Nov. 2010.

&lt;http://www.exopaedia.org/Pleiades&gt;.

"Pleiades (star cluster)." *Wikipedia*. N.p., 19 Oct. 2010. Web.

29 Oct. 2010.

&lt;http://en.wikipedia.org/wiki/Pleiades_%28star_cl

uster%29&gt;.

"The Pleiadians - Alien Races." *Uncensored News*. N.p., 7

Aug. 2009. Web. 1 Nov. 2010.

&lt;http://newsuncensored.blogspot.com/2009/08/pl

eiadians-alien-races.html&gt;.

"The Pleiadians Speak." *Memes.org*. N.p., n.d. Web. 1 Nov.

2010. &lt;http://memes.org/pleiadians-speak&gt;.

Prout, Susan. "Angel Dictionary." *Angelic Reflections*. N.p.,

n.d. Web. 4 Nov. 2010.

&lt;http://www.angeldrawings.com/angelDictionary/a

ngelsK.html&gt;.

Raines, Ken. "Jehovah: Ancient Astronaut from the

Pleiades?" *The Forbidden Knowledge*. N.p., n.d.

Web. 4 Nov. 2010.

&lt;http://www.theforbiddenknowledge.com/hardtrut

h/jehovah_astronaut.htm&gt;.

Royal, Lyssa, and Keith Priest. "An Excerpt from: The Prism

of Lyra An Exploration of Human Galactic Heritage."

*Royal Priest Research.* N.p., n.d. Web. 4 Nov. 2010.

<http://www.lyssaroyal.com/book1ex.htm>.

Russell, Charles Taze. *Thy Kingdom Come.* Allegheny:

Watch Tower Bible and Tract Society, 1908. Print.

Simonsen, Mike. "Ophiuchus - the 13th Sign of the Zodiac."

*Simostronomy.* N.p., 31 Mar. 2010. Web. 4 Nov.

2010.

<http://simostronomy.blogspot.com/2010/03/ophi

uchus-13th-sign-of-zodiac.html>.

Smith, J. G. *Angels and Women.* New York: A. B. Abac

Company, 1924. *Internet Archives.* Web. 4 Nov.

2010.

<http://ia310805.us.archive.org/3/items/AngelsAn

dWomen/1924_Angels_and_Women.pdf>.

Smith, William. *Dictionary of Greek and Roman antiquities.*

London: Taylor and Walton, 1848. Print.

- - -. *A dictionary of the Bible: comprising its antiquities,*

*biography, geography, and natural history.*

Hartford: S. S. Scranton & Co., 1896. Print.

Theosophical Publishing Society, London. "Numbers, Their

   Occult Power and Mystic Virtues." *Lucifer, A*

   *Theosophical Magazine* 5 (1890): 322-323. Print.

*Theosophical Siftings - Volume Six.* London: Theosophical

   Publishing Company, 1893. Print.

Theosophical Society. "Theosophical Religion." *Theosophical*

   *Review* 32 (1903): 20. Print.

"The Truth about the Pleiadians." *Steelmark.* N.p., n.d. Web.

   1 Nov. 2010.

      <http://www.steelmarkonline.com/pleiadians.htm>

"Vega in Fiction." *Wikipedia.* N.p., 30 Oct. 2010. Web. 4

   Nov. 2010.

      <http://en.wikipedia.org/wiki/Vega_in_fiction>.

Von Bunsen, Ernst. *The angel-messiah of Buddhists,*

   *Essenes, and Christians.* London: Longman, Green

   and company, 1880. Print.

Wells, Junius F. "Nigh Unto the Throne of God." *The*

   *Contributor: representing the Young men's and*

   *Young ladies' mutual improvement associations of*

   *the Latter-day saints* 1889: 158. Print.

"Who Are The Pleiadians?" *Pleiadian Realm.* N.p., n.d. Web.

  1 Nov. 2010.

    <http://www.pleiadians.net/WHO_ARE_THEY_/w

    ho_are_they_.html>.

Wolpert, Stuart. "Planets forming in Pleiades star cluster,

  astronomers report." *UCLA Newsroom.* University

  of California at Los Angeles, 14 Nov. 2007. Web. 29

  Oct. 2010.

    <http://www.newsroom.ucla.edu/portal/ucla/rocky

    -planets-are-forming-in-the-40289.aspx>.

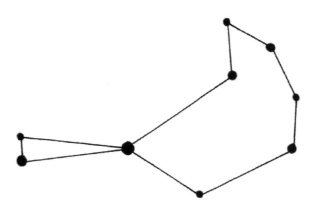

## INDEX

## About the Author

Living part-time in the U.K. and Ireland, and the rest of the year in the U.S., Dace Fitzgerald Allen lives an adventurous (albeit low-profile) life as a researcher and author.

For more information, see PleiadiansFiles.com

## For further reading

This is the first of at least two books planned for the Pleiadians Files series.

The second book is scheduled for publication in 2011.

Volume Two will focus on Pleiadian connections to Vril energy, Hollow Earth Theory, UFOs, and other topics of science and controversy.

# The Pleiadians Files

## PleiadiansFiles.com

Made in the USA
Charleston, SC
09 November 2010